Howard, Henry

England's Newest Way in All Sorts of Cookery, Pastry, and All Pickles

ISBN: 978-1-948837-14-9

This classic reprint was produced from digital files in the Google Books digital collection, which may be found at http://www.books.google.com. The artwork used on the cover is from Wikimedia Commons and remains in the public domain. Omissions and/or errors in this book are due to either the physical condition of the original book or due to the scanning process by Google or its agents.

This edition of Henry Howard's **England's Newest Way in All Sorts of Cookery, Pastry, and All Pickles** was originally published in 1726 (London).

Townsends
PO Box 415, Pierceton, IN 46562
www.Townsends.us

John Clark ejus Liber
1735.

John Clark

Ejus Liber

1765

b = 61
7
b 4
0 ε

Mithridate 47 + 0 - 2 = 52

ENGLAND's

NEWEST WAY in all

SORTS

OF

COOKERY, PASTRY,

AND

All PICKLES that are fit to be used.

ADORNED

With Copper Plates, setting forth the Manner of placing Dishes upon Tables; and the Newest Fashions of Mince-Pies.

By HENRY HOWARD,

Free Cook of *London*, and late Cook to his Grace the Duke of *Ormond*, and since to the Earl of *Salisbury*, and Earl of *Winchelsea*.

To which is added,

The Best Receipts for making Cakes, Mackroons, Biskets, Ginger-Bread, French-Bread: As also for Preserving, Conserving, Candying and Drying Fruits, Confectioning and making of Creams, Syllabubs, and Marmalades of several Sorts.

Likewise, Additions of Beautifying Waters, and other Curiosities.

As also above Fifty new Receipts are added which renders the whole Work compleat.

The FIFTH EDITION.

LONDON:

Printed for J. Knapton, R. Knaplock, J. and B. Sprint, D. Midwinter, B. Lintot, A. Bettesworth, W. and J. Innys, J. Osborn, R. Robinson and A. Ward. 1726.

TO THE

READER.

THIS *small Treatise having met with such Reception and Encouragement, that Four Impressions of it have gone off within the Space of a few Years; I have made it my particular Care and Study to find out such other Receipts excellent in their Kind, as may tend to the further Improvement of those that are curious in the necessary and commendable Art of* Cookery. *An Art, which for the Variety of Subjects it is concerned in, the many various*

Shapes

To the Reader.

Shapes it appears in, infinuating itfelf to almoft every one of our Senfes at one and the fame Time, adminiftring Delight with Profit, and for the Honour it has to be employed in the Service of Perfons of the firft Rank and Quality, is little inferior to any other Art whatfoever.

Befides thefe, I have here added for the Sake of that better Part of Mankind, the Fair Sex, feveral choice Receipts for making Beautifying-Waters, Oyls, Ointments, and Powders, to render the Features of a Face more lively, its Complexion clear and beautiful; and to cleanfe it from Morphews, Pimples, Sunburn and Freckles: That they may be enabled to affift themfelves on all neceffary Occafions, without having Recourfe to idle prating Goffips, or other quack Pretenders; who with Mercurial Fucus's cheat them of their Beauty as well as Money.

The Receipts you find added in this Edition are fingularly good in their refpective Kinds, extracted out of Choice Manufcript of feveral Ladies who were

par-

To the Reader.

particularly Excellent in Cookery *and
Beautifying the Face. As for those in
the former Edition, I need not say much
the Name of the Author,* Mr. Howard,
*is a sufficient Character for them, besides
the speedy Vent of Four Impressions. The
Book is not stuff'd with a Multitnde of
insignificant Receipts to make it bulky,
that was beyond my Intent, which was
not too appear great, but to please and
profit; and by these New Additions, to
express my grateful Respects for the
kind Reception the former Impressions
met with, have therefore taken care that
the Receipts be rather good than many.*

*Every particular Art hath its pro-
per Terms and certain Rules and Me-
thods, which through disuse are easily
lost and forgot. The Memory, like po-
lished Steel, the more it is used, the
brighter the Reflection, but neglected,
rusts and dulls. This Manual therefore will be a necessary Companion to
several Persons to refresh their Memo-
ries of those Excellent Things which
they shall at any time happen to for-
get, as well as to present such Rari-*

A 3 *ties*

To the Reader.

ties of *Art* to them, as they were never before acquainted with. *An Alphabetical Table methodically digested at one easie View, readily presents the Reader with the valuable Contents, and directs them to the Pages.* I shall add no more, but humbly submit my self, and the Book to the Candid Judgment of the Judicious Artists.

Note, The CONTENTS of the Additional Receipts, are at the latter End of the BOOK.

A

THE
TABLE.

A.

B.

A 2   Beef

The TABLE.

A

The TABLE.

Currant-

The TABLE.

The TABLE.

The TABLE.

L.

The TABLE.

L.

M.

Marmalade

The TABLE.

A

The TABLE.

Oyster-

The TABLE.

To

The TABLE.

The TABLE.

The TABLE.

S.

To

The TABLE.

Tongues

The TABLE.

V.

W.

The TABLE.

W.

I N D E X

TO THE

Additional Part.

A

The INDEX.

                                            For

The INDEX.

ENGLAND's

Neweſt Way of

COOKERY.

Of Puddings.

1. *Italian Pudding.*

TAKE a Pint of Cream, a penny white Loaf, ten Eggs, a beaten Nutmeg; butter the Bottom of your Diſh, and round the Sides: Then cut twelve Pippins in round Slices, and lay in the Bottom; throw a little Orange-peel over them, and ſome fine Sugar; pour half Pint of Claret over them, and then the Pudding; make Puff-paſte over it, and it will be baked in half an Hour; lay the Paſte round the Sides of your Diſh.

B   2. *Pip-*

2. *Pippin Pudding.*

Take twelve Pippins, boil them tender, and scrape them clean from the Core, and put in a Pint of Cream, season'd with Orange-flower, or Rose-water and Sugar to your Taste; and put good Puff-paste in your Dish; bake it in a flack Oven, grate Loaf-sugar over, and send it.

3. *Orange Pudding.*

Take two right Sevil Oranges; take off a little of the out-side Rind, and squeeze out the Juice and Seeds, lay them in Water three Days, shifting the Water every Day: Then set on a Pot of Water, make it boil, and put them in a Mortar, and beat them into a Paste; then put in double their Weight of double refined Sugar, eight Eggs, leave out half the Whites; then boil a Pint of Cream, set it to be cold, and put them in with three or four Spoonfuls of Sack; grate the Quantity of a Half-penny Roll, and put in, with half a pound of sweet Butter melted, sweeten it to your Taste, and put it into a Dish with Puff-paste round it, and it will require no more baking than a Custard.

4. *Carrot Pudding.*

Take a large Carrot, boil it tender; then set it by to be cold and grate it through a hair Sieve very fine, then put in half a pound
of

of melted Butter, beaten together, with eight
Eggs; leave out half the Whites, with two
or three Spoonfuls of Sack, or Orange-flower
Water, half a Pint of good thick Cream, a
Nutmeg, grated Bread, and a little Salt:
Make it the Thickneſs of the Orange Pudding, and the ſame baking; ſweeten it to
your Taſte with fine Sugar, make Puff-paſte,
grate Sugar over it, and ſend it.

5. Oat-meal Pudding.

Take a Pint of fine Oat-meal, boil it in
New Milk and Cream, a little Cinnamon
and Nutmeg, and beaten Mace, and when
it is about the Thickneſs of a Haſty-pudding,
take it off, and ſtir in half a pound of ſweet
Butter, and eight Eggs (leave out half the
Whites) very well beaten, and put in two
or three Spoonfuls of Sack, and make Puff-
paſte, and lay round your Diſh, and butter
it very well, and bake it, but not too much;
ſend it.

6. Rice Pudding.

Take half a pound of Rice, boil it in New
Milk till it is ſoft and tender; then ſet it by
to be cold, and cover it cloſe; then grate
one Nutmeg, one Penny-worth of Mace
beaten, ten Eggs, leave out half the Whites,
with two or three Spoonfuls of Sack, or
Orange-flower Water, a Pint of Cream;
ſweeten it to your Taſte with good fine

B 2   Sugar,

Sugar, melt a pound of freſh Butter, and mix all theſe together with the Rice, when cold; then ſhread a quarter of a pound of Mutton or Beef-ſuet, ſtrow it a top, and it will make it look with an Icen; then make Puff-paſte and lay in the bottom of your Diſh, and three quarters of a pound of Currans will do for this Quantity, plump your Currans before you put them in; but it is genteeler without Currans; ſtrow Sugar over it, and ſend it to your Ladyſhip's Table for a Pudding that I like.

7. Marrow Pudding.

Take a Quart of Cream, and boil it with a Blade of Mace, ſet it to be cold a little: Then beat ten Eggs, leaving out half the Whites, and put to your Cream; then cut a penny Loaf into Slices, and lay a Layer of Bread, and a Layer of Marrow with a few Raiſins of the Sun; and ſo do till you have laid out your penny Loaf, and three quarters of a pound of Marrow: Then ſweeten your Cream and Eggs, and put in two Spoonfuls of Orange flower-water: pour it over your Bread with a thin Puff-paſte in the bottom, and round the ſides of your Diſh; ſend it.

8. Excellent Pudding.

Take a Quart of Cream, boil it with two Manchets, and grate in one Nutmeg, ſix Yolks and four Whites of Eggs well beaten,

with

with your Bread and Cream at leaſt half
an Hour together; then put into it a pound
of a Beef-ſuet finely minced, half a pound
of Sugar, a little Salt, bake it three quarters of an Hour in a quick Oven, the ſame
way boiled without Suet as long, is as
good.

9. *Good Pudding.*

Take a penny white Loaf, pare off all the
Cruſt, and ſlice it thin into a Diſh with a
Quart of Cream, ſet it over a Chaffin-diſh
of Coals, till the Bread be almoſt dry; then
put in a piece of ſweet Butter, and take it
off and let it ſtand to be cold; then take the
Yolks of three Eggs, the White of one with
a little Roſe-water, Sugar and Nutmeg;
ſtir them very well together; then put it in
another Diſh, butter it, and when it comes
out of the Oven, grate over it fine Sugar;
ſend it.

10. *Good Pudding.*

Take grated Bread, as much Flour; then
take four Eggs, two Whites, a good quantity of Sugar, wet it with Cream to the
Thickneſs of Pancake-batter; then put in
ſome Raiſins of the Sun, and butter your
Diſh very well, and bake it half an Hour,
ſtrow over it grated Sugar, and ſend it to
the Table.

11. *Good Pudding.*

Take a Quart of Cream, put to it a pound of Beef-fuet cut fmall, feafon it with Nutmeg, Rofe-water and Sugar: Then grate two Manchets, and beat feven Eggs, put in half a pound of Currans; mingle all thefe well together, butter the Difh, and bake it not too much; grate Sugar over it.

12. *Green Pudding.*

Take fome boiled Mutton minced, with Beef-fuet fhreded, a little Thyme, Marjoram and Parfly, and a handful of Spinage; then mix all thefe together with a little grated Bread, and three Yolks of Eggs, fome Cream, Sugar and Nutmeg, Currans, and a little Flour; then rowl it up in a Sheep's Caul; bake and fend it.

13. *Calves-Foot Pudding.*

Boil two pair of Calves-feet very tender, and fet them by to be cold; then cut the Meat off and mince it very fmall; then flice a penny Loaf and fcald a Pint of Cream, fhred fix Ounces of Beef-fuet very fine, with five Yolks and two Whites of Eggs well beaten, a good handful of Currans, Nutmeg, Sugar and Salt; then fold a Caul of a breaft of Veal like a fheet of Paper, leaving one end open, fill it with the Pudding, and a good quantity of Marrow, fow it up

in

in a Cloth and boil it almoſt two Hours;
then take it up and lay it on Sippets with
Verjuice, Butter and Sugar, ſtick it with
blanched Almonds, Orange and Citron-
peel; you may put in Sack inſtead of Verjuice if you pleaſe.

14. *Puddings to boil Chickens or Pidgeons with.*

Take the Fleſh of a Rabbet, or the Wing
of a Capon, for want of theſe a piece of
Veal or Lamb with the Kidney-fat, or Mar-
row-ſuet, or both, as much Meat as Suet;
ſhred them as ſmall as you can with Parſley,
Thyme, Savory, and Marjoram, ſeaſon it
with Cloves, Mace, a little Salt, and put to
it three Spoonfuls of grated Bread, mingle
them with Cream and the Yolk of an Egg;
then pare the Fleſh with your Fingers from
the Legs and Necks, and put in ſome of the
Pudding, fill them not too full leaſt they
ſhould break in boiling; then boil them in
Milk and Water with a bunch of ſweet
Herbs, and a blade of Mace, and a little Salt;
then beat ſome Butter with the Juice of an
Orange with the Butter; ſend it.

15. *A Cabbage Pudding.*

Take half a pound of Veal, ſhred it with
two pound of Suet very ſmall, grate two
Nutmegs with a pretty quantity of Pepper
and Salt; then take Cabbage half boiled as
much as will lie on a Sawcer; then take ſe-

ven

ven Eggs beaten very well, and mingle up
all together like a Pudding; then put it in a
Cloth, boil it well, and send it up.

16. *Quaking Pudding.*

Take a Pint of very thick Cream, eight
Yolks of Eggs and two Whites, beat them
very well with a little Rose-water, mingle
the Eggs with the Cream, then grate in
some Nutmeg, sweeten it to your Taste, and
flower a Bag very well, put it in and tye it
fast, and so put it into a Pot of boiling Water, and keep it boiling continually; and
when it is boiled enough turn it out of the
Bag, and make your Sauce of Sack, Butter
and Sugar, and pour all over it with Orange,
Limon, and Citron-peel; cut them thin,
with Almonds blanched and cut in little
Pieces, and stuck upon it.

17. *Shaking Pudding of Almonds.*

Take a Pint of Cream, boil it with a blade
of Mace, strow it over with some beaten Almonds, a little Orange-flower or Rose-water;
then take four Eggs, leave out two Whites,
strain the Cream, Eggs and Almonds together; then take some Sugar and sweeten it,
and thicken it with grated Bread or Bisket;
then take a Cloth and rub it with Flour, and
tye it up and dip it into Rose-water; then
boil it, and when it is boiled eat it with Butter, Sugar and White-wine, stick it with
blanched Almonds; send it.   18. *Al-*

18. *Almond Pudding.*

Take a Quart of Cream, two Eggs, beat them and ſtrain them into the Cream, and grate in a Nutmeg and a penny-Loaf, ſix ſpoonfuls of Flour, half a pound of Almonds beaten fine together, mix them and ſweeten it with good fine Sugar; then flower the Bag and boil it, and when it is boiled enough melt Butter with a little Orange-flower, or Roſe-water beaten thick with a little Sack, and pour it on the Pudding, and ſtick it with blanched Almonds; ſend it.

19. *Almond Pudding.*

Take two Loaves of white Bread grated very fine, put to it four Yolks of Eggs, and half a Pint of Cream, and a quarter of a pound of blanched Almonds beaten very fine in a Mortar, with two or three ſpoonfuls of Sack or Orange-flower-water, ſome Marrow and Beef-ſuet cut ſmall, a little Nutmeg, and ſweeten it to your Taſte; then tye it up in a Pudding-Cloth and boil it; then ſend it.

20. *Haſty-Pudding.*

Take a Pint of Milk and put to it a handful of Raiſins of the Sun, as many Currans; then take a Manchet, grate it, and put in a little Flour and Nutmeg, and let it boil a quarter of an Hour; then put in a piece of Butter in the boiling, and diſh it with pieces
of

of Butter laid up and down upon it, then
fend it to the Table.

21. *Almond Pudding in Guts.*

Take a pound of Almonds, beat them with
Orange-flower-water to prevent their Oyling; then take twelve Eggs with half their
Whites, a little Salt, four Nutmegs, beat
them together with two pound of Beef-fuet
finely fhreded; then take one pound and an
half of Sugar, and eight penny Loafs finely grated and fearced with half a Pint of
Orange-flower-water, and a Pint of Cream:
When you have mixed thefe together fill the
Guts, but not too full left they fhould break.
Dip the Guts in Rofe-water when you fill
them, and Marrow is better than Suet if you
have it, then boil them not too long.

22. *White Pudding.*

Beat half a pound of Almonds with Rofe-
water very fine; then take as much Ox-pith
out of the Skin, and beat with the Almonds;
then boil a Quart of Cream, and beat fome
of it with the Pith and Almonds a while;
and put in two grated Nutmegs, and grate
two Naple-biskets, and a Grain of Musk and
two of Amber-greafe, and grind it with the
Sugar before you mix them with the things:
put in ten Eggs, leave out four Whites, with
the Marrow of three or four bones cut pretty
big, a pound of Sugar, fome candied Citron
cut

cut fmall, and boil them enough ; fet them
by for ufe.

23. *White Puddings.*

Take a pound of Naple-bisket, cut it into
pieces, and grate a penny Loaf; then boil a
Quart of Cream and put to the Bisket and
Bread to fwell them ; take a pound of blanched Almonds, beat them fmall ; then take
two or three fpoonfuls of Orange-flower or
Rofe-water to keep them from Oyling: Put
in eight Eggs, leave out four Whites, with
fome beaten Nutmeg and Mace, the Marrow
of eight Bones, half of it cut fmall, and the
other half in pretty pieces to put in as you
fill them ; then cut in fome Citron and a
little Amber-greafe, a little Salt, fill them
but not too full; give fcope enough, fweeten
them with good fine Sugar, and Bullocks is
beft to fill them dipt in Rofe-water.

24. *Black Puddings.*

Take a Pint of Oat-meal, and put to it
eight Pints of New Milk, fteep it all Night,
or boil it to the Thicknefs of Pudding ; then
put it to eight Pints of grated Bread and four
Eggs, a little Salt, and a little Cloves and
Mace, fome Sage and Penny-royal, fome
fweet Herbs, mix them together well: Then
take a Pint and half of Blood, and ftrain it
into it, and if it be not foft enough put in
fome more Milk into it with half a pound of
Beef-

Beef-suet finely shredded : Cut one pound
and an half of Lard into long Pieces; then
fill them and give them one boil ; then take
them up, and with a Pin prick them to give
them vent ; then put them in and boil them
till they are full enough, and you may put in
Cream instead of Milk if you please.

25. *Liver Pudding.*

Boil a Hog's Liver, dry it in an Oven after Bread, dry it enough to grate ; then sift
it through a coarse Sieve, and take half a
pound of it to a pound of grated Bread, and
a pound of Currans, two pound of Beef-suet
kept dry, and cut small, and sifted thorough
the same coarse Sieve ; season it to your
Taste with one Ounce of Spice, which must
be Cinnamon, Cloves, Mace, Nutmeg, and
two Grains of Amber grease ; then mingle
all these together as you do Minced pye, and
boil three Pints of New Milk, pour it into
all these things ; then cover it a while, and
beat six Eggs with two or three Spoonfuls of
Orange-flower-water ; mix them well together and put in a little Salt, you may put
in Rice pap, instead of grated Bread.

26. *Carp Pye.*

Take a couple of Carps or Tench, then a
great Eel, or according to the Quantity you
make ; skin it and bone it, mix it with a
good quantity of grated Bread, and a few
sweet

fweet Herbs, with the Yolks of hard Eggs; and after, take Anchovies and about a handful of Oyfters, and cut them all very fmall; then feafon it pretty high with Salt, Pepper, Cloves, Mace, Nutmeg, and a little Ginger, four or five Yolks of hard Eggs, and half a pound of Butter, work it together as you do your Pafte; then after cut your Carps in three or four Pieces; then fill their Bellies with forc'd Meat, and feafon your Carps with thefe things, Herbs and Spice, fo put them in the Pye, and what it won't hold lay in Bales about it with Oyfters, and Butter about them, and then clofe it up and put it in the Oven, and let it ftand an hour and a half; after it comes out, take three or four Eggs, and beat them very well and put them in, give them a fhake or two; fend it.

27. *Salmon Pye.*

Make Puff-pafte and lay in the bottom of your Patty-pan; then take the middle Pieces of Salmon, feafon it high with Salt, Pepper, Cloves and Mace, cut it into three Pieces; then lay a Layer of Butter and a Layer of Salmon till it is laid all out; then make forced Meat of an Eel, and chop it fine with the Yolks of hard Eggs, with two or three Anchovies, Marrow and fweet Herbs, a little grated Bread, a few Oyfters, if you have them; lay them round your Pye, and on the Top; feafon them with Salt and Pepper, and other Spices as you pleafe.   28. *Po-*

28. *Potatoe Pye.*

Boil the Potatoes, peel them and lay them in the Pye with good store of Marrow, whole Mace, preserved Lettice-Roots and Stalks, and Citron cut: Cover it with Butter, and when it comes out of the Oven scald White-wine and put some Sugar in, and give it a shake or two, and send it.

29. *Artechoke Pye.*

Boil your Artechokes well; then take the Bottoms from the Leaves, and season them with a little beaten Mace, and put to them a pretty Quantity of Butter, lay a Layer in the bottom; then lay in the Artechokes; sprinkle them with a little Salt, put some Sugar over them, put in grated Pieces of Marrow rowled up in the Yolks of Eggs; then put in a few Gooseberries or Grapes, and lay upon it large Mace and Dates ston-ed, some Yolks of hard Eggs, Suckets, Lettice-stalks and Citron; cover it with Butter, and when it is baked, put in scalded White-wine, and shake it together; send it.

30. *Egg Pye.*

Boil sixteen Eggs, take the Yolks, cut them small, and put to them three or four spoonfuls of Orange-flower-water, with the same quantity of Sack, season it with Cloves, Mace, Nutmeg, and fine Sugar to your Taste,

and

and lay a Layer of wet and dry Sweet-
meats ; then melt a pound and a quarter of
fweet Butter, beat it with half a Pint of
Cream ; then mix all thefe Ingredients together, and put it in the Pye and bake it, and
when it is drawn, fcald a little White-wine
and beat it with the Yolk of an Egg, Sugar
and grated Nutmeg, pour it in and give it a
fhake or two ; fend it.

31. *Lumber Pye.*

Take the Humbles of a Deer, parboil them,
and clear all the Fat from them ; then put
as much Beef-fuet as Meat, or half as much
more, as you like it ; mince it together very fmall, and feafon it with Cloves, Mace,
Nutmeg, Cinnamon and a little Salt, half a
pound of Sugar, three or four pound of Currans, a Pint of Sack, a little Rofe-water,
half a pound of candied Orange, Limon
and Citron-peel, and Dates ftoned and fliced, fill your Pye and clofe it ; and when
it is baked put in half a Pint of Sack, or
more ; fend it.

32. *Stump Pye.*

Take a Leg of Lamb from the Bones, and
mince it fmall, with a good Quantity of
fweet Herbs, and a good Quantity of Currans, grated Nutmeg and Salt ; feafon it to
your liking, and mix it with two or three
Yolks of Eggs beat with Sack or White-wine ;

then

then lay it clofe in the Pye, and lay on the Top either Fruit or Sweat-meats; do not bake it too much, and when it is baked cut it up, and put in Verjuice and Sugar, or White-wine; make it hot before you put it in, then lay on the Lid; fend it.

33. *Dowlet Pye.*

Take Veal parboil'd or roafted, and cut it fmall, with Sweet-herbs and Beef fuet; then put fome into it feafon'd with Sugar, Nutmeg and Cinnamon if you like it; then beat as many Eggs as will wet it; then make it like Eggs, and ftick a Date in the middle of each of them, and lay them in a Pye, and put fome dried Plumbs over them, and if in Time of Year put in ripe Plumbs; then take White-wine, Sugar and Butter, and pour it in a little before you draw it, fcald the Wine, and give it a fhake or two together; fend it.

34. *Calves-Foot Pye.*

Take Calves-feet and boil them tender; then cut them in halves, and take out all the Bones, and lay a Layer of Butter in the bottom of the Pye; then a Layer of Calves-feet; then Raifins of the Sun ftoned and cut fmall; then lay a Layer of Calves-feet; then Raifins of the Sun ftoned and cut fmall, Currans, Limon, Orange and Citron-peel cut into thin flices, a little beaten Cloves, Mace, Nut-

Nutmeg, a little fine Sugar, and a little Salt; mix all thefe together, and lay a Layer till it is all laid óut; then boil fix Eggs, take out the Yolks and cut them into pieces, and ftrow them a Top with a Layer of Butter; don't make it greafie; fend it.

35. *Chicken Pye.*

Take young Chickens, feeth them ìn half Milk and Water, ftrip their Skins from them, butter your Difh and put Puff-pafte round it, and in the Bottom; then lay a Layer of Butter, and a Layer of all forts of wet Sweet-meats, and dry, then trufs up your Chick-ens with their Heads on; feafon them with Cloves, Mace, Nutmeg, Salt, and a little good Sugar; then rowl up their feafoning in a piece of Butter and put in their Bellies, and lay them in the Pye with a good Layer of Butter over them, and Sweet-meats, then lay on the Lid being made of Puff-pafte, and an Hour will bake it; take care your Oven is not too hot, it being apt to rafh and lofe Colour.

36. *For the Caudle.*

Take half a Pint of White-wine or Syder, boil it with a blade of Mace, and a little Nutmeg; then take it off the Fire, and put in the Yolks of two Eggs very well beaten, with a fpoonful of Sugar and a little bit of Butter rowled up in the Flour; then let

C   it

it run thorough a Tunnel through the Hole on the Top of the Pye whilſt the Pye is hot: Give it two or three Shakes; ſend it up.

And if for a ſavory Pye; Put in Muſhrooms inſtead of Sweet-meats, with Artichoke-bottoms, Cocks-combs and Pullets, Veal Sweetbreads ſet in Water and pulled in pieces; make good Puff-paſte for your Patty-pan, and lay a Layer of theſe with Force-meatballs, and a Layer of Chicken ſeaſoned with Salt, Pepper and Spice, with a bit of Butter in their Bellies rowled up with Seaſoning, and Butter on the Top; and if in time of Year put in Gooſeberries and ripe Currans, bake it and put in the ſame Caudle, only leave out the Sugar; give it two or three Shakes when you ſend it.

37. *For the Force-meat-balls.*

Take Chicken-marrow, or a little Thyme and Savory, a few Crumbs of White-bread, with the Yolks of two Eggs well beaten, ſeaſon it with Salt, Pepper, Cloves and Mace, then ſcald a little Spinage, drain it well, and cut it ſmall and put it in, and mix it well together to make them look Green; make ſome long and ſome round.

38. *Hare Pye.*

Take a Hare, dreſs him; take one part and mince it ſmall with Bacon, Thyme, Savory

vory and Marjoram; feafon it with Salt,
Pepper, Cloves, Mace and Nutmeg; and
when you have drefs'd the other part feafon it as you did the firft; work your minced
Meat with the Yolk of an Egg or two, and
lay it about your Hare, and fill it up with
fweet Butter and clofe it, bake it not too
much; and when it is baked put in half a
Pint of ftrong Gravy, and give it a Shake
or two; fend it.

39. *Jiblet Pye.*

Take young Jiblets and fcald them, put
them on the Fire and ftew them very Tender; feafon them with Salt and Pepper pretty high, with a bunch of fweet Herbs, an
Onion, and juft Water enough to cover them;
then take them out of the Liquor and let
them ftand to be cold; then put them in
your Patty-pan with good puff-pafte round
it, and put in what quantity of Butter you
think fitting, with the Yolks of hard Eggs,
and lay over it Force-meat-balls; and when
you have lidded your Pye leave a Hole a
Top, and juft as it goes into the Oven, put
in half the Liquor that the Jiblets was ftewed in; bake it not too much; fend it up.

40. *Venifon Pafty.*

Take three quarters of a peck of fine Flour,
and put fix pound of Butter in the Flour;
then beat in twelve Eggs, and make your

C 2   Pafte

Pasty with warm Water; bone the Venison, beat and break the Bones, season it with Salt and Pepper to fill up the Pasty when it comes out of the Oven; then season your Venison with an Ounce and half of black Pepper just bruised, and Salt; then take about a pound of Beef-suet, cut it into long Slices, beat it with your Rowling-pin, and strew over it Salt and Pepper; then lay the Venison on the Top, season it very high with Pudding-crust round the Pan, and put in a large Porringer of Water, and lay a Layer of good fresh Butter and cover it; shake your Pasty, and when it comes out of the Oven pour in the Liquor that you made of the Bones, and shake it well together; serve it to the Table.

41. *To season Turkey, Goose or Pigeons.*

Bone them, or break their bones very well; season them with Salt, Pepper and Nutmeg, if you like, within and without; stick some whole Cloves in their Breasts, fill them with Butter and put them in your Coffin, and lay Butter all over the Top; then close it and bake it four Hours; when it is baked fill it up with clarified Butter: A cold Dish.

42. *To season Veal or Lamb.*

Take a Loin of Veal or Lamb, cut it into small Pieces, season it with Nutmeg, Salt and Pepper; then fill the Pye and lay some Butter

ter on the Top; then clofe it and bake it;
and if you ferve it up hot, put in a Pint of
Gravy; but if you keep it cold put in more,
but fill it up with clarified Butter.

43. *To feafon Mince-Pyes.*

Take the beft part of a Neats-tongue, a
little more than half boil it; then peel it,
and cut it into Slices, fet it to be cold; then
weigh it, and to a pound of Tongue put a
pound and half of Beef-fuet and Marrow;
then put your Meat and Suet upon a Chop-
ping-block, and chop it very fine and mix
it well together; then weigh a pound of
Meat to a pound of Currans; pound your
Spice, which muft be Cloves, Mace and Nutmeg; feafon it to your Tafte with a little
fine Sugar, Orange, Limon and Citron-peel
thin fhred, with two or three Pippins hack'd
fmall; wring in the Juice of a Limon, and
put in a large Glafs of Claret, and as much
Sack, a few Dates ftoned and fliced thin, a
few Raifins ftoned and cut fmall; mix all
thefe things very well together; then fill
and lid your Pyes; bake them, but not too
much.

44. *Olive Florendine.*

Take the beft part of a Leg of Veal; cut
it into thin Slices like *Scotch* Collops, beat
them on both fides with the back of a Knife;
feafon them with Cloves, Mace, Pepper and

Salt;

Salt; then cut a pound of fat Bacon into thin Slices, rowl them up one by one, with a slice of Veal in the Middle; then put them in a Dish, and put to them three or four Anchovies, two or three Shalots, half a handful of Oysters, and half a hundred of Forcemeat-balls, a Limon sliced with the Rind off; put in half a Pint of White-wine, half a Pint of strong Broth, a little Gravy, and half a Pound of Butter; cover it with Puffpaste and bake it.

45. *Stake Florendine.*

Take a Leg or a Neck of Mutton, cut it into Stakes; season it with Nutmeg Pepper and Salt: Put it into a Dish with three or four Shalots, a bunch of sweet Herbs, two or three Anchovies, twenty Balls of Forcemeat, half a Pint of Claret, as much fair Water; put in half a pound of Butter, cover it with Puff-paste; bake it.

46. *Rice Florendine.*

Take half a pound of Rice picked clean, boil it first in Water, then in Milk, till it be as thick as Hasty-pudding; then set it by till it is cold; then beat in six Eggs, leave out half the Whites, put in half a Pint of Cream, two or three Spoonfuls of Sack, a little Rose-water; season it with two Penny-worth of Cloves, Mace, Nutmeg and Cinnamon, half a pound of Sugar, a little Salt, a pound of Currans, four Ounces of candid Orange, Limon and Citron-peel, a pound of Marrow or Butter; then cover it with Puff-paste, and bake it; the same Ingredients for Almond Florendine, only blanch the Almonds, and beat them in a Stone Mortar with a Glass of Sack, and a little Rose-water, and you may garnish your Dish with Paste-Royal.

47. *Almond-Florendine.*

Take one pound of Jordan Almonds blanched and beaten in a Mortar, with a little Orange-Flower-water; take the Yolks and half the Whites of eight Eggs beat with a quarter of a pint of Sack, half a pint of Cream, half a pound of fresh Butter melted, a pound of Currans, as much Sugar as will sweeten it to your Taste, a quarter of a pound of Marrow seasoned with beaten Cloves, Mace and Nutmeg; you may put in candid Limon and Citron-peel : Mix it well together, make Puff-paste on the Top and Bottom, and bake it in a slack Oven, not too much.

48. *A Florendine.*

Take what quantity of Curds you please, turn them the same way as for Cheese-cakes; put in a pound of blanched Almonds beat very fine, with a spoonful of Rose-water, half a pound of Currans, as much Suggar as

will

will fweeten it; then take a good quantity
of Spinage; let it have two or three boils,
then drain it, and fhred it fmall, mingle it
together, butter your Difh; ferve it.

49. *To feafon Cheefe-cakes.*

Take a Gallon of New-Milk warm from
the Cow, fet it with a fpoonful of Runnet;
as foon as it comes, ftrain the Runnet from
the Curds; rub them through a little Range
with the back of a Spoon; feafon them with
half a quarter of an Ounce of Cloves, Mace
and Cinamon beat fine, a little Salt, half a
pound of Sugar, a little Rofe-water, half a
pint of Sack, half a pound of Butter melted
thick; beat in fix Eggs, leave out half the
Whites, put in a pound of Currans, and it
is fit for ufe.

The fame Ingredients for Rice-cakes, only
you muft boil the Rice tender before; the
fame way for Almond-cakes, only beat
them in a Stone Mortar, with a Glafs of
Sack, and a little Rofe-water.

50. *To feafon Cuftards.*

Boil a Quart of Cream with a blade of
Mace, or a little broken Cinnamon, a little
Nutmeg fliced thin; ftrain it and feafon it
with half a pound of Sugar, a little Sack
and Rofe-water; then beat in eight Eggs,
leave out half the Whites, harden the Crufts
before you fill them. It muft be good fine
Sugar,

51. *Paſte Royal.*

Take a pound of very fine Flour; put in a little Cinnamon and Nutmeg very fine beaten, a quarter of a pound of very fine double refined Sugar, beat in the Whites of ten Eggs; then make it into a Paſte with half a Pint of Sack, and the beſt Cream pretty ſtiff; then rowl in a pound of Butter at five or ſix times rowling; this is fit for Orange-Puddings, Spread-tarts and Laid-tarts, or to garniſh Diſhes with.

52. *White Puff-paſte.*

Take a pound of fine Flour, put in the Whites of three Eggs beaten up; make it into Balls with cold Water; then rowl in a pound of Butter at five or ſix times rowling; it is fit for Taffata-tarts or Cheeſe-cakes; in the Winter beat your Butter to make it work, and in the Summer keep it as cool as you can.

53. *Puff paſte.*

Take three great handfuls of Flour well dried: Put to it two Whites of Eggs, and a quarter of a pound of Butter; wet it with cold Water; then take three quarters of a pound of Butter, divide it into three Parts, rowl the Paſte abroad, and ſtick on a quarter of a pound of Butter in little bits all over it, ſo fold it up again and flour it; then
rowl

rowl it abroad again, and fo do three times
till the Butter is ended; then butter the
brims of a Difh and lay the Pafte thereon;
put it prefently into the Oven; let it bake
almoft an Hour; this quantity is but enough
for the brims of a Difh ; if you would have
enough to cover it all over a Difh, you muft
take as much more of every thing, and make
a double Quantity.

54. *To drefs Fifh : Craw-Fifh.*

Take Craw-fifh boiled in Water with a
little Salt, and when they are boiled enough
take them up, and fet them to be cold ;
then pick the Meat out of the Legs and the
Tails, fet it by; then take the Bodies and
Claws, beat them in a Mortar with fome of
the Liquor they were boiled in, and to a
Quart of that Liquor add a Quart of Cream,
and a Quart of Milk: Put in a blade of
Mace, a Nutmeg cut into Quarters, with a
Clove or two ; fet them all over the Fire,
and boil them well ; then take a little Sorrel
and Spinage a little beat, and Leeks a large
handful altogether ; cut them large, and
put them in with your Craw-fifh that you
picked out ; let them boil together, but
don't let your Herbs lofe their Colour ; then
put in a *French* Loaf and place that in the
middle of your Difh, and juft when you
fend it in thicken it with the Yolks of Eggs
and a piece of frefh Butter, a quarter of a
pound ;

pound; take care your Eggs don't curdle, and let it be the thicknefs of good Cream; ferve it.

55. *To Stew Carps.*

Stick your Carp as you do a Pig, and fave all the Blood you can; fcale it and take out the Ruffage; take care you don't break the Gall: Then take as much Claret and ftrong Gravy as will cover him in your Stew-pan, a little White-wine and Salt, a good piece of Horfe-radifh, and a bunch of fweet Herbs, fome whole Pepper, Cloves and a little Mace, with a large Onion, fome Mufh-rooms and Capers; let them ftew together till they are enough; then brown fome But-ter with Flour, and pour fome of the Li-quor to the Butter, with two or three An-chovies chopt fmall; then have in readinefs Oyfters fried; fqueeze in the Juice of a Li-mon: Garnifh with Horfe-radifh, fried-Parfly, Oranges and Limons.

56. *To ftew Eels.*

When they are half ftewed, put to them a bunch of fweet Herbs, a little grated Bread, and Onion, fome beaten Mace and Cloves, as it boils; and when they are al-moft enough, put in a little Butter, and a Glafs of Claret with an Anchovy; then take it up.

57. *To stew Oysters.*

Set on the Fire a Pint of Oysters with their Liquor, a Shallot, half a Pint of White-wine, a little white Pepper, three blades of Mace, a little Salt to season it, a piece of sweet Butter, let them stew softly, till they are enough, about half an Hour; then put in another piece of Butter, shake it together, and when it is melted, lay Sippets in the Dish; serve them for a Side-dish.

58. *Sauce for Fish.*

Take a little Thyme, Horse-radish, Limon-peel, some whole Pepper; boil them a little while in fair Water; then put in two Anchovies, and four spoonfuls of White-wine; let them boil a little; then strain them out and put the Liquor into the same Pan again, with a pound of fresh Butter; and when its melted take it off the Fire, and stir in the Yolks of two Eggs, being well beaten before, with three spoonfuls of White-wine; set it on the Fire again, and keep it stirring till it's the thickness of Cream, then pour it on your Fish very hot, and serve it.

59. *To Butter Crabs.*

Take out the Meat and cleanse it from the Skins; put it into a Sauce-pan with a quarter of a Pint of Sack, or White-wine, an Anchovy, a little Nutmeg, and Crumbs
of

of White-bread, set them on a gentle Fire,
and beat them together for Dishing; then
stir in the Yolk of an Egg, and a little Pepper well beaten; then stir them well together, so put it into your Shell again : Send
it for a Side-dish.

60. *To Butter Shrimps.*

Stew a Quart of Shrimps with half a Pint
of White-wine, with a Nutmeg, then beat
four Eggs with a little White-wine, and a
quarter of a pound of beaten Butter; then
shake them well in a Dish till they be thick
enough; then serve them with one Sippet
for a Side-dish.

61. *Oyster Leaves.*

Take *French* Rowls, cut a little Hole on
the Tops as big as a Half-Crown; then take
out all the Crumb, but don't break the
Crust off the Loaf; then stew some Oysters
in their own Liquor, a blade of Mace, a little whole Pepper, Salt, Nutmeg, and a little
White-wine; scum it very well, and thick-
en it with a piece of Butter rowled up in
Flour; then fill up the Rowls with it, and
put on the piece again that you cut off;
then put the Rowls again in a Mazerene-
Dish, and melt Butter and pour it into them,
set them in your Oven till crisp; let the
Oven be as hot as for Orange-pudding.

62. *T*

62. To Dress a Cod's-Head.

Take a large Cod's-Head with the Neck
cut large, feafon the Pickle that you boil it
in; then put in a good handful of Salt,
whole Pepper, all Spice, a little Limon-peel,
a Bay-leaf, an Onion, a Pint of White-wine,
and Water enough to cover it: When thefe
are well boiled together put in your Cod's-
Head, and let it be well boiled: Then take
it up and put it in a Difh over your Stow to
draw the Water from it, and have all things
ready: Garnifh with Horfe-radifh and fliced
Limon.

63. To boil Pike.

Put a living Pike, fcowre the infide and
outfide very well then wafh him clean, and
have in readinefs a Pickle made of Vinegar,
Mace, whole Pepper, a bunch of fweet Herbs,
and fome Onion: and when the Liquor boils
put in the Pike, and fo order it, that the
Pike may boil: as foon as the Pike is ready,
(and half an Hour will boil a Pike a Yard
long) make your Sauce: take half a Pint of
Sack, beat into it a Crab, a Lobfter and
Shrimps: then draw a Pound of Butter,
two fpoonfuls of Liquor, mingle all thefe
together, and fet them on your ftow, and
ftir them all the while till it be thick: pour
the Sauce over the Pike, which muft be firft
difhed upon Sippets dipt in the Broth: fcrape
some

some Horse-radish in the Sauce, and put in some Craw-fish ; send it.

64. *To roast Pike.*

Take a large Pike, scrape and scald it, take out the Guts: then season it with Salt, Pepper, Cloves, Mace and sweet Herbs, rub it all in very well: take a large Eel, bone and cut it in square Pieces, as if it was Bacon, season it with the same of your Pike, rowl the Pike in the Caul of a Breast of Veal, and tye it to the Spit, and when its half roasted take off the Caul and dridge it with grated Bread, baste and flour it, then roast it well, and Yellow: Garnish your Dish with raspt Limon and Flowers.

65. *To roast an Eel.*

Take a great Eel, slit the Skin a little way, then pull off the Skin, Head and all, then parboil the Eel till it comes from the Bone, then shred it with some Oysters, sweet Herbs, Limon-peel, season it with Salt, then scowre the Skin with Water and Salt, then stuff it full again with the Meat, sow it up and roast it with Butter, then take for Sauce some White-wine, dissolve three Anchovies in it, then beat as much Butter as will serve for Sauce : serve it.

66. *To roast Lobsters.*

Take your Lobsters and tye them to the Spit alive, baste them with hot Water and
Salt,

Salt, and when they look very red, and you think they are ready, baste them with Butter and Salt, then take them up and have your Sauce ready, and put into Plates round your Dish.

67. To *Malaret Soals.*

Take the largest Soals you can get, wash, skin and dry them, beat them with your Rowling-pin, then take as many Yolks of Eggs and Flour as will dip them on both Sides: Then have your Frying-pan ready, then put in as much sweet Oil as will cover your Fish, and fry them brown, and as yellow as Gold; then take them up and lay them upon a Fish-plate to drain, when they are cold make your Pickle thus: Take Salt, Pepper, White-wine Vinegar, Cloves, Mace and Nutmeg, boil it all together well: Let the Liquor be put into a broad Earthen-pan, that your Fish may lie at full length in it five Days: Garnish with Limon-peel, Fennel and Flowers; serve it.

68. To *Pickle Lobsters.*

Boil your Lobsters in Salt and Water, till they will slip out of their Shells, take the Tails out whole, make your Pickle half White-wine, and half Water, put in whole Cloves, whole Pepper, two Bay-leaves, Mushrooms, Capers, a Branch of Rosemary, with a little Cucumber, put in your Lobsters:

sters : Let them have a boil or two in the
Pickle, take them out, set them by to be
cold, let the Pickle boil longer, and put in
the Bodies, for that will give them a pretty
Relish : When the Lobsters and Pickle are
both cold, put them in a long Pot for
Use.

69. *To pickle Oysters.*

Take the largest Oysters you can get, set
the Liquor on the Fire with a good deal of
Mace, a Race of Ginger, whole long Pepper, a little Salt, three Bay-leaves, an Onion, boil these well together, then put in
your Oysters, and let them boil a quarter
of an Hour ; then take out your Oysters,
put them in the Pot you intend to keep them
in ; let your Pickle have a boil or two ; take
it off, set it by to cool ; then put your Oysters in a long Pot for Use.

70. *White Soop.*

Take four pound of coarse Beef, three
pound of Mutton set it on the Fire with seven Quarts of Water, let it boil very flow ;
scum it clean, and let it boil two Hours ;
then take the Meat up in a Tray, take up a
little of the Liquor and beat out all the
Goodness of the Meat, and put in the Liquor
again ; cut off a pound of each piece to put
in the middle of your Dish ; then take two
Spoonfuls of Oat-meal, ten Corns of white

D   Pepper

Pepper and a little Salt, a quarter of a pound of Bacon, a Carrot, a Turnip cut in pieces; then put in half your Soop-herbs, which muſt be Sorrel, a little white Bete, hard Lettice, a Leek, the quantity of two handfuls in all; cut them groſs, and put in half at ten a Clock with the Liquor, and about eleven put in the reſt, ſo let it boil till twelve; then take it off and put it in your Soop-Diſh, with the pieces of Meat in the Middle; let it ſtand over the Stow till one a Clock, then cut in a half-penny Roll at ſix ſlices, and take five Yolks of Eggs and beat them, and take up a little of the Liquor and put to the Eggs and beat and ſtir them well into the Soop; then garniſh with brown Cruſt grated round the brims of your Diſh.

71. *Brown Soop.*

Take a large Neck of Veal, a Neck of Mutton, half a pound of middling Bacon, a blade of Mace, three Cloves, ſome whole Pepper and Salt, a bunch of ſweet Herbs, an Onion; let theſe boil gently in a little more Water than will cover them; and when all the Goodneſs is boiled out, take it up and ſtrain the Broth from the Meat; then cut two pound of Beef in Pieces, beat and flour it; and put a piece of Butter in your Pan, and let it boil up in the Pan; fry it brown, put in the Liquor you ſtrained from the Meat, and you may put in two Ducks, which
you

you muſt half roaſt before you put them in; and when they are ready put them in the middle of your Diſh, with a handful of Spinage and Sorrel cut pretty big, and let them ſtew till they are enough, and put in Cockscombs, Palats and Sweet-breads pulled in pieces, Truſſels and Troffes if you can get them; ſtir it in, and put in a little fried criſp Bread.

72. *Good Soop.*

Take a Leg of Beef, a Knuckle of Veal, the fat End of a Neck of Mutton; let them be chopt to pieces, and make Broth of them, with a Cruſt of Bread; then cleanſe the Broth from the Meat, and put it into an Earthen-pot, and put in a Pint of Whitewine, with a bunch of ſweet Herbs, with good ſtore of Spinage; then take a Hen, lard it with Bacon, and boil it in the Broth, and when it's enough pour it in a Diſh, with the Juice of an Orange, and beat as many Yolks of Eggs as will thicken it, and keep it ſtirring about for fear it ſhould curdle; then put your Fowl in the middle of your Diſh with the Broth and Sippets; ſerve it.

73. *White Broth.*

Take a Pullet, boil it, and when you think it's enough, take it up and put it into a Diſh; then boil your Cream with a blade of Mace,

D 2 and

and thicken it with Eggs ; then put in the
Marrow of one Bone, and take ſome of the
Broth and mingle it together ; put to it a
ſpoonful of White-wine, let it thicken on
the Fire ; and put the Pullet hot out of the
Broth, and ſet it on Chafing-diſh of Coals
and ſend it.

74. *Peaſe Soop.*

Make ſtrong Broth of a Leg of Beef, ſet
it by to be cold ; then ſet it on the Fire with
two Quarts of Peaſe, let them boil till they
be enough, with an Onion ſtuck with Cloves
then ſtrain it into another Pot, and ſet them
on the Fire again ; ſeaſon it pretty high with
Salt, Pepper, Spice, and all ſorts of Soop-
herbs, Spinage, Sorrel, Lettice, young Betes,
a large Leek with bits of Bacon cut in the
Diſh, and put in a Pint of ſtrong Gravy,
with Forc'd-meat-balls, criſpt Bread, and
criſpt Baçon ; ſerve it. You may put in the
middle of your Diſh eight larded Pigeons,
and roaſt is as proper as boiled : Garniſh
with grated Cruſt of Bread and criſpt Baçon ; ſerve it.

74. *Peaſe Pottage.*

Take eight pints of Peaſe, and ſix quarts of
Water ; ſet them on the Fire together with
a large Onion, ſeaſon them high, let them
boil ; and when they are enough, ſtrain
them through a Cullendar, and ſet them on
the

the Fire again; and when they are boiled,
put in four handfuls of Spinage, two Leeks,
a little Mint, two spoonfuls of Flour tem-
pered with Water; then put in your Forc'd-
meat-balls, and a little after a pound of
sweet Butter; keep it stirring till the Butter
is melted; then dish it to the Table; don't
cut the Herbs small but grofs; take care
they don't lose their Colour; serve it.

76. *Plumb Pottage.*

Take a Leg of Beef, and a Neck of Mutton; put 'em in four Gallons of Water, let
'em boil till all their Goodness is out; then
take it off the Fire and strain out the Meat
from the Broth, and when it's cold take off
all the Fat, and the next Day make your
Broth, and grate the Crumb of a Six-penny
Loaf, and let it steep in a little of the Liquor an Hour; then set your Liquor on the
Fire, and put in two Nutmegs cut into quarters, with some whole Mace, four Cloves,
break in a little Cinnamon; put in a pound
of Currans two pound of Raisins of the Sun,
and half a pound of Dates stoned; put in
the Bread with the Fruit, and season to your
Taste, and put in a Bottle of Claret, a Pint
of Sack, and tye up a few Plumbs and Prunes
in a Rag, and plump them, and grate a
brown Crust of Bread round the brims of
your Dish, with some of the Plumbs laid in
heaps all round, here and there a heap.

77. *Beef Alamode.*

Take a fleshy piece of Beef; take out the Fat and Skins, and Carse; then beat it well, and flat it with your Rowling-pin or Cleaver, lard it with fat Bacon quite through as long as your Meat is deep, and as big as your Finger; then season it high with Salt, Pepper, beaten Nutmeg, Cloves and Mace; then put it into a Pot where nothing but Beef has been boiled in good strong Broth, and put in a handful of sweet Herbs, a Bay-leaf, so let it boil till 'tis tender, then put in a Pint of Claret, three Anchovies, and let them stew till you find the Liquor taste well, and the Meat tender; and if there be more Liquor than will make an end of stewing then take as much of it up as you think fit, before you put in your Wine and other things; then put all the things in, and let it stew till you see the Liquor do thicken, and taste well of the Spice; then take it up, and take out the Bay-leaves and Shalot; you may eat it hot or cold.

78. *The Olea.*

Take twelve Pigeons, six Chickens; pull the Pigeons, dry them, and put them in whole; scald the Chickens, cut them in halves; then half roast a Rabbit, and cut it into pieces as long as ones Finger; boil a Neats-tongue very tender, cut it in thin

pieces

pieces as big as half Crowns, with Sweetbreads pulled in little pieces : Put to all this Meat one Quart of Claret, and three Pints of ſtrong Gravy, let it ſtew ſoftly with the Meat; put to it a little whole Pepper, four whole Onions, Thyme, Savory and Marjoram tied up in a bunch; let all theſe ſtew together till the Meat is almoſt enough; then put in a good many Capers ſhred ſmall, twenty pickled Oyſters with three ſpoonfuls of their Liquor, four blades of large Mace, the Peel of a Limon ſhred, and a Limon and half cut into pieces as big as Dice; mingle all theſe well together; then beat twelve Eggs into the Liquor, let them ſcald in it to thicken it; rub the Diſh you intend to ſerve them in with Garlick; then build the Meat up in an heap and pour the Liquor all over it; then lay upon the Meat Marrow, being firſt boiled, Oyſters fried, Limon ſliced, Mace, Sauſages criſpt, Bacon and Balls made of grated Bread, a little Cloves, Mace, Salt, and a few Marigolds ſhred; wet them with the Yolks of Eggs, and rowl them in Balls, and boil them before you lay them on; cut them if you pleaſe, and lay them on the Meat with blanched Beans, and Frenchbeans; ſerve it.

79. *A Hogooe.*

Take a Leg of Mutton, take off the Skin whole, with the upper Knuckle; then take

D 4 the

the Flesh, with a pound of Beef-suet, and shred them very fine; take some Spinage, a little Thyme and Savory, small Shalots, shred them small; put in some Salt and Pepper; then take six Yolks of Eggs, work the Meat and all together very well into a great Ball; then take a Cabbage and open the Leaves, and cut a hole to put in the Meat, and shape it long-ways, like the Body of a Duck, and boil a Duck's Head, and stick it on with a Skewer; then bind the Body close, and tye it up hard; then boil it well, and have in readiness some Sausages fried, and dipt in the Yolks of Eggs, with a little Flour and Nutmeg, a good deal of Butter, with some Anchovies dissolved in the Sauce first, and beat up with the Butter and Pickles; serve it.

80. *A Monastick.*

Take a Quart of Rice, two quarts of strong Gravy; set it on the Fire very high, and let it stew soberly, but not boil; then put in an Onion stuck with Cloves, and a bunch of sweet Herbs; then put in a large Pullet, fill the Belly with Forc'd-meat and Oysters, with half a pound of Bacon; let these stew together till it's tender, and about the Thickness of Hasty-pudding; then put in the Forc'd-meat-balls that you have fried: and some you must stew with it; then take it up and beat the Yolks of three Eggs, and

about

about a quartern of Butter rowled up in Flour, and shake them well together, and the Juice of a Limon ; then dish it with the Fowl in the middle, and the Bacon with Forc'd-meat-balls round it : Garnish with Limon, and grated Bread round the brims of your Dish, and serve it.

81. *Scotch Collops.*

Take a Leg of Veal, cut off as much of it as you think fitting into thin slices ; beat it with your Rowling-pin ; scratch it with a Knife ; lard it with Limon-peel, Bacon and Thyme ; then take sweet Marjoram, Savory, Parsly, young Onions, Salt, Pepper, a little Nutmeg ; shred them fine, and rub the Meat very well with them ; then dip the Meat in Yolks of Eggs, and a little Flour ; fry them in a little fresh Butter, and when they are fried enough take them out of the Pan, and have ready a little strong Gravy, and dissolve in it some Anchovies, a Glass of Claret, and a Shalot or two, and a Limon wrung into it, with some shred upon it : Let it stew between two Dishes, and beat a piece of Butter with the Yolk of an Egg, and thicken it up, and pour it over your Meat, with crispt Bacon, fried Oysters, Mushrooms, Veal Sweat-breads pulled in little pieces, with Forc'd meat-ball : Garnish with Horse-radish and Barberries ; serve it.

82. *To*

82. *To dreſs a Calve's Head.*

Boil the Head till the Tongue will peel;
then cut half the Head into ſmall Pieces, a-
bout the bigneſs of Oyſters; lay the Brains
by themſelves; then ſtew it in ſtrong Gravy,
with a large Ladle full of Claret, and a handfull of ſweet Herbs, a little Limon-peel, a
piece of Onion and Nutmeg ſliced; let all
theſe ſtew till they are tender then take the
other half of the Head, ſcratch it a-croſs,
ſtrow over it grated Bread, ſweet Herbs, with
a little Limon-peel; lard it with Bacon, and
waſh it over with the Yolks of Eggs, and
ſtrow over it a little grated Bread; boil it
well over Charcoal, or Wood-coal: and
when it's enough place it in the middle of
your Diſh; then cut the ſtewed Meat, and
put in a Pint of ſtrong Gravy into your Stew-
pan, with three Anchovies, a few Capers, a
good many Muſhrooms, and a good quantity of ſweet Butter, with a Quart of large
Oyſters; ſtew them in their own Liquor,
with a blade of Mace, a little White-wine;
keep the largeſt out to fry, and ſhred a few
of the ſmalleſt; then beat the Yolks of Eggs
and Flour, and dip them in; fry them in
Hog's Lard; make little Cakes of the Brains,
and cut the Tongue out into round pieces,
and dip them in and fry them, then pour
the ſtewed Meat in the Diſh round the o-
ther half of the Head, and lay the fried Oyſters,

fters, Brains and Tongue with little bits of
crifpt Bacon, Force-meat Balls, or Saufages
on the Top, and all about the Meat : Garnifh with Horfe-radifh and Barberries ; ferve
it up hot.

83. *Frigafee of Rabbets or Chickens.*

Take Rabbets or Chickens, only you muft
skin the Chickens ; then cut them into fmall
pieces, beat them with your Rowling-pin ;
then lard them with Bacon, and feafon them
with Salt, Pepper, and a little beaten Mace,
then put in half a pound of Butter in your
Pan, brown it, and dridge it with Flour,
and put in your Rabbets, and fry them
brown ; and have ready a Quart of good
ftrong Gravy, Oyfters and Mufhrooms, three
Anchovies ; a Shalot or two, a bunch of fweet
Herbs, a Glafs of Claret, feafon it high ;
and when they are boiled enough, take out
the Herbs, Shalot and Anchovy-bones ; fhred
a Limon fmall and put in ; and when your
Rabbets are almoft enough, put them in, and
let them ftew all together, keeping them fho-
ving and fhaking all the time it's on the Fire ;
and when it's as thick as Cream take it up,
and have ready to lay over it fome bits of
crifpt Bacon, fome Oyfters fried in Hog's
Lard to make them look brown ; dip them
in the Yolks of Eggs, and Flour, and a little
grated Nutmeg, and Force-meat-balls : Garnifh with Limon and Flowers ; ferve it.

84. *For*

84. *For the Forc'd-meat-balls.*

Take Rabbet, Veal or Pork; fhred it very fine, with a few Chives, fweet Herbs, and a little Spinage to make them look Green: feafon them with Salt, Pepper, Mace, Anchovies, Marrow or Beef-fuet; cut all thefe very fine together, and bind them with a little Flour, and the Yolk of an Egg, and rowl up fome long, fome round; fry them brown and crifp, or ftew them as you pleafe.

85. *Frigafee White.*

Parboil your Chickens; then skin them, and cut them into pieces, and fry them in ftrong Broth, with a blade of Mace, a little Salt and Pepper, two Anchovies, two Shalots; let them fry till they are enough; then take out the Shalots, and put in half a Pint of good Cream, and a piece of Butter rowled up in Flour, and the Yolk of an Egg; ftir it all about till it is as thick as Cream; wring in the Juice of a Limon, take care it don't curdle it; then fcald a little Spinage, cut it and throw over it fome Mufhrooms, a few Capers fhred with Oyfters, if you have them, with a little of their Liquor; then ferve it to the Table on Sippets.

86. *Frigafee of Pigeons.*

Take eight Pigeons new killed, cut them into fmall pieces, and put them into a Frying

ing-pan with a pint of Claret, and a pint of Water; feafon, your Pigeons with Salt and Pepper; then take a little fweet Marjoram, Thyme, a few Chives, or an Onion; fhred the Herbs very fmall, and put them into the Frying-pan to the Pigeons, with a good piece of Butter; fo let them boil gently, till there be no more Liquor left than will ferve for the Sauce; then beat four Yolks of Eggs, with a Spoonful and half of Vinegar, and half a Nutmeg grated; when it's enough, put the Meat on the one fide of the Pan, and the Liquor on the other. Then put the Eggs into the Liquor on the Fire, and ftir it till it's the Thicknefs of Cream; then put the Meat into the Difh, and pour over the Sauce; lay crifpt Bacon and fried Oyfters over it, and garnifh with rafpt Limon; ferve it.

87. *Frigafee of Mufhrooms.*

Take the largeft and biggeft Mufhrooms you can get, and fome fmall ones amongft them; Cut the largeft into four pieces, peel them and throw them into Salt and Water, let them lie in the Water and Salt half an Hour; then take them out and put them into a Bell metal or Silver-skillet, and ftew them in their own Liquor, with a little Cream, to make them look white, and cut hard; lefs than half an Hour will ftew them; then ftrain them out into a Sieve, and take a quarter of a Pint of that Liquor they were ftewed

ed in, with as much White-wine and strong
Gravy, boil all these together with a little
whole white Pepper, Mace and Nutmeg, two
Anchovies, one sprig of Thyme, a Shalot or
two; season it very high to your Taste, with
these things; when it has boiled well together, strain out the Spice, Anchovy-bones
and Shalot, and put it into your Stew-pan
again with the Mushrooms to it, and have
ready the Yolks of three Eggs, with the
quantity of as much Butter as an Egg rowled
up in Flour, and beat it well with a spoonful
of Cream, and so shake it up together, the
Mushrooms, and all very thick, so that it
may hang about the Frigasee, and scald a
little Spinage and shake over it; serve it.

88. *To force a Leg of Mutton.*

Take a large Leg of Mutton, cut a long
slit in the back-side, then take out all the
Meat you can get, but don't deface the Meat
on the other side, then take your Meat and
chop it fine, with three Anchovies unwash-
ed, a little beaten Mace and Nutmeg, a few
Chives or an Onion, a little Limon-peel and
sweet Herbs, Salt, Pepper and Oysters, a
good deal of Marrow or Beef-suet; then put
all these in your Mortar, and beat them all
together very fine, then stuff in your Meat
again, and stitch it up with good strong
Thread to keep your Meat in; then put it
it into a Dish, and wash it over with the Yolks
of

of Eggs to bind it, and dridge it with Flour,
and lay pieces of Butter all over it; bake it
or roaft it, and it's very good; then have
ready Oyfters ftewed in White-wine, with a
blade of Mace, keep out the largeft to lay
with Anchovy-fauce, Mufhrooms and a good
Quantity of ftrong Gravy; ferve it.

89. *The fame way force a Leg of Lamb.*

And make a Frigafee of the Loin to lay
round about it, cut into fmall pieces pretty
thin; feafon it with Salt, Pepper, beaten
Cloves, Mace and Nutmeg, a few fweet
Herbs and Chives, then fry it in clarified
Butter, and when it's fried enough pour the
Butter out, and wipe the Pan clean, and put
in a Pint of ftrong Gravy, a quarter of a Pint
of White-wine or Sider; then let your Lamb
ftew in the Gravy; then throw in fome
Mufhrooms, a few Oyfters, with the Liquor,
an Anchovy; then rowl up a piece of Butter
in Flour, and the Yolk of an Egg, and
fqueeze in the Juice of a Limon: Garnifh
with Limon and Pickles.

90. *Veal Alamode.*

Take a large Philet of Veal, cut out the
Bone, and the hard Skin; then take Salt, Pepper, Cloves and Mace, pound the Spice and
mix them together; then take Thyme, Marjoram, Shalot, Limon-peel; fhred them very fmall, and mix them with the Seafoning;
then

then take half a pound of Bacon, cut off the
Rind and Ruſty, and cut it out into thick
pieces as thick as your Finger, and as broad
as two Fingers, and rowl it up in the Seaſoning, and skewer it up cloſe, and tye it
in the ſame faſhion as it was before you cut
it; then beat the Yolks of Eggs and waſh
it all over, and put it into a Diſh to bake,
with pieces of Butter all over it; and when
it comes out of the Oven, take the Veal out
and ſerve it, and if you pot it, tye it over
with double Cap-paper, and put in two
pound of Butter, keep back the Gravy, and
if it be not covered, clarify as much Butter
as will cover it; and as you want it cut it
out into Slices, eat it with Oil and Vinegar
beat up thick together, or the Juice of a
Limon, or what you pleaſe.

91. *To Ragow a Breaſt of Veal.*

Take a large Breaſt of Veal, more than
half roaſt it; cut it out into four pieces, and
have ready as much ſtrong Gravy as will cover it; put it into your Stew-pan, ſeaſon it
high with Pepper, Cloves, Mace, Nutmeg, a
little Salt, Shalot, Limon-peel, Muſhrooms,
and Oyſters fried and ſtewed, Sweet-breads
ſet and skinned, and pulled in little pieces;
and when it's enough, fry your largeſt Oyſters with criſpt Bacon, and Forc'd-meat-
balls, and for a White Ragow take the ſame
Ingredients, only boil the Breaſt of Veal in
half

half Milk and Water; with a bunch of sweet
Herbs, a little Limon-peel, Mace, whole
Pepper, and two Bay-leaves; then, when
it's enough, wash it over with the Yolks of
Eggs, and a little Butter, and put it in your
Stew-pan, just long enough to make it look
Yellow, and thicken your Sauce with the
Yolks of Eggs, and a piece of Butter rowled
up in Flour, with three spoonfuls of Cream
thickned up together.

92. *To Ragow a Neck of Veal.*

Cut a large Neck of Veal into Stakes, beat
them flat with your Rowling pin; then season with Salt, Pepper, Cloves, Mace, lard
them with Bacon, Limon-peel and Thyme;
dip them in the Yolks of Eggs, then take a
large Sheet of Cap-paper, turn it up at the
four Corners like a Dripping-pan, and pin it
tight; Butter it, and rub the Gridiron with
Butter; then put on your Meat over a Charcoal Fire; let it do leisurely, keeping it basted and turning to keep in the Gravy; and
when you think it's enough, have ready as
much strong Gravy as you think will do,
season it pretty high, and put in some Mushrooms, with all sorts of Pickles, some stewed and fried Oysters, and Forc'd-meat-balls
dipt in the Yolks of Eggs, and Flour, to lay
round, and a top of your Dish; send it. And
if for a brown Ragow, put in Claret. If for
a white, put in White-wine, with the Yolks

E   of

of Eggs, beat up with three spoonfuls of
Cream : And you may put in a young Fowl,
or a larded Feasant, with Forc'd-meat in
the Belly, or larded Pigeons : Garnish with
Limon and Barberies ; and serve it.

93. *To Ragow Pigeons.*

Take Pigeons, lard them, and cut them
into Halves, and do some whole ; season
them with Salt Pepper, Cloves and Mace ;
wash them over with the Yolks of Eggs ;
and take a good deal of Butter and put into
your Frying-pan, and brown it with a little Flour ; then put in your Pigeons, and
just brown them ; then take them out, and
put in your Stew-pan as much strong Gravy
as will cover them ; let them stew till they
are very tender, with a bunch of Sweet-
herbs ; aud when they are almost enough,
take out the Herbs and put in the Anchovies, Oysters, and what Pickles you have,
with a little Shalot ; then roast Larks, or
what small Birds you have to lay round
your Dish ; and for want of Birds, fry
Sweet-breads ; set them pulled in pieces,
dipt in the Yolks of Eggs : Garnish with
Orange and Pickles ; send it.

94. *Beef Royal.*

Take a Surloin, or a large Rump of the
best Beef ; bone it, and beat it very well ;
season it with Salt, Pepper, Cloves, Mace,
Nutmeg,

Nutmeg, and a little Limon-peel, Savory,
Marjoram, and a little Thyme; then make
ftrong Broth of the Bones, and lard the Meat
quite through, with large pieces of Bacon;
then put in a good deal of fweet Butter in
your Stew-pan, and brown it; then put in
the Meat, and brown it on both fides; then
put in the Liquor with the Butter, with two
Bay-leaves, fix Truffels and Troffees, if you
have them, and Pallets for want of thefe,
put in Sweet-breads pulled in pieces; cover
it down clofe; let it ftew till it's tender; then
take it out and fcum off all the Fat, and put
in a Pint of Claret, with three Anchovies;
then put in the Beef to be thoroughly hot,
and put in what Pickles you have, with fried
Oyfters; thicken up the Sauce, and pour
over your Meat; fend it. It's very good
cold, but it's a noble Difh hot.

95. *To* Malaret Fowls.

Take Pullet, Chicken, or Veal Sweet-
breads, Mufhrooms, Oyfters, Anchovies,
Marrow, and a little Limon-peel, a little
Pepper, Salt, Nutmeg, and a little Thyme,
Marjoram and Savory, a few Chives: Mingle all thefe with the Yolk of an Egg, then
raife up the Skin of the Breaft of your Fowls,
and ftuff it, and then ftich it up again, and
lard them; fill their Bellies with Oyfters,
and roaft them; make good ftrong Gravy-
fauce;

ſauce: So you may do Feaſants, Turkeys,
or what Fowls you pleaſe.

96. Geeſe *Alamode*.

Take two Geeſe, and raiſe their Skins as
before, and make your Stuffing as for the
Fowls; only inſtead of Chives, put in two
Cloves of Garlick; ſeaſon high, and put in
ſome into their Bellies, as well as between
their Skins; lard them with Limon and
Thyme; then put in as much Butter in your
Stew-pan as will brown them on both ſides;
then put them in the Butter with ſtrong
Gravy, ſeaſoned very high; and when they
are ſtewed enough take them out; thicken
the Sauce with Butter, rowled up in Flour,
and the Yolks of Eggs, with half a Pint of
Claret, and let them boil to be thick; then
fry Oyſters and Forc'd-meat-balls, and criſpt
Sippets to lay round your Diſh, and ſerve
it: Garniſh with grated Bread, and Flowers round your Diſh.

97. *To* Pickle *Tongues.*

Make your Pickle with Salt-petre, and
Sal-prunellæ; and to ſix Quarts of Water,
one Ounce of each, a Pound of Bay-ſalt,
the ſame of White-ſalt, and a quarter of a
pound of brown Sugar; then boil all theſe
together 'till the Scum riſes, and is a very
ſtrong Brine; skim it clean; and when it's
cold, put your Tongues in a Tub; let them
lie

lie at their full length to be covered; turn
them three times a Week, and in three Weeks
they will be fit to boil; then peel then, and
eat them with Chicken or Pigeons, and Spar-
row-grafs, Colliflowers, Cabbage, Spinage,
or what is in feafon, and it's a noble Difh,
and you may keep them in the Pickle as
long as you pleafe, and rub them with Bran,
and hang them up in your Chimney, to eat
cold; get the beft Tongues.

98. *Leg of Mutton like Weftphalia-Ham.*

Take a Leg of Mutton, cut into the fhape
of a Weftphalia-Ham, and make the Pickle
of two parts Salt-petre, and the other Bay-
falt: Let it lie in Pickle three Weeks; then
take it out and hang it in a fmoaky Chimney
as you do Bacon, and lay under it a Wifp
of Hay, which you may fet on fire to fmoak
your Leg with; and when it's dried, and
you intend to boil it, put it into a great Kettle with a good deal of Hay, having fome
Hay-feeds in a Bag in the Kettle: You may
eat it hot, with Fowls, or cold, like Weftphalia-Ham, as you pleafe.

99. *To Hafh a Calve's-Head.*

Take a Calve's-Head, and half boil it;
cut it into pieces, and take a Pint of great
Oyfters with half a pound of Butter, and
large Mace, a bunch of fweet Herbs; and
take half a Pint of White-wine, fome An-

E 3   chovies,

chovies, and put it in between two Diſhes,
and ſtew it tender, and boil the Brains with
Sage and Parſly by themſelves; then put
Scotch-Collops in the Bottom of your Diſh
with bits of fried Bacon, and a good piece
amongſt the Meat, with a quantity of Marrow boiled, with blanched Almonds, and
Cheſnuts, the Yolks of hard Eggs, ſome
fried Sauſages, and rowl up a large piece
of Butter in Flour, and thicken it up with
Butter, and lay the Bacon and Oyſters a
Top, and round about; ſerve it up hot to
the Table.

100. *To Haſh a Leg of Mutton.*

Cut off the Fleſh of a Leg of Mutton, into broad Pieces, neither Fat nor Skin; beat
it with the back of a Chopping-knife, but
not to pieces; then put it into a Diſh raw,
it being firſt rubbed with Garlick, and put
Liquor into it with a whole Onion cut in
the middle, a little bunch of ſweet Herbs
tyed up, and ſome Salt; cover it, and let it
ſtew 'till it be changed from the Colour of
the Blood; then put in a quarter of a Pint
of White-wine, three blades of Mace, an
Anchovy, and let it ſtew ſo much longer,
'till the Anchovy be diſſolved; Then take
out the Onion and Herbs, and put the Meat
and Liquor into the Diſh; and ſerve it.

101. *To Hash a Shoulder of Mutton.*

Take a Shoulder of Mutton, half roast it, then cut it as thin as you can, and take a Glass of Claret, a blade of Mace, two Anchovies, a few Capers, a Shalot, Salt, a sprig of Thyme, Savory and Limon-peel ; let it stand half an Hour covered ; and when it's enough, shake over it some Capers, and serve it.

102. *To Stew a Neck of Mutton.*

Cut it into Stakes, wash it, season it with Salt, Pepper and Nutmeg ; cover it with Water, and put it in a Stew-pan ; when it boils scum it well, and let it stew : Then take your Turneps, Carrots and Cabbage, parboil them ; strain 'em from the Water ; when your Meat is half stewed, put in the Roots, throw in a handful of Capers, and a handful of sweet Herbs, a handful of Spinage and Parsly ; shred them together, with two Anchovies chopt ; take a little Butter, and brown it ; shake in a little Flour take a Ladle full of the Broth, and put in the Butter that is browned, let it boil up, and pour it over your Meat, when it's almost ready, boil it a little up together, and serve it with Sippets in the Bottom of your Dish ; squeeze in the Juice of a Limon, or an Orange ; serve it.

103. *To Stew Veal.*

Cut the Veal into little pieces, ftew it in Water, put a little Butter in it, feafon it with Salt, whole Pepper, Mace, a little Limon-peel, an Onion; let your Liquor quite cover it, fo ftew it; and when it's enough beat the Yolks of Eggs, and ftir them in; then let them have a warm or two; and if your Veal is dreffed, you may heat it this way.

104. *To Stew Chickens.*

Take Chickens, quarter them, and put them into White-wine and Water, but moft Wine; and when they are ftewed tender, put in a good quantity of Butter, and a bunch of fweet Herbs, with large Mace; then take the rafping of a Manchet to thicken it, with a good quantity of Parfley; you may put in a little Sage, if you like it, a little Salt, Pepper and Nutmeg to feafon your Chickens; then lay Marrow on the top of them, with the Yolks of Eggs well beaten, with the Juice of a Limon in the Sauce: Garnifh with fliced Limon and Parfly, and ferve it to the Table.

105. *To Stew Pigeons.*

Melt a good quantity of Butter, mingle it with Parfly, Sorrel and Spinage, which you muft ftew in fome Butter; and when it's

cold

cold put some into their Craws, with a Bay-leaf, save some of it for Sauce ; then stew the Pigeons in as much strong Cravy as will cover them, with some Cloves, Mace, Salt, Pepper, and Winter-savory, a little Limon peel, a Shalot or two; then brown some Butter and put in ; and when they are stewed enough put in a little bit of Butter rowled up in Flour, and the Yolk of an Egg, with some of the Herbs you left out; shake it up all together, and send it.

106. *To dress a Shoulder of Mutton in Blood.*

When you kill your Mutton save the Blood; take out all the Knots and Strings, and let it steep five Hours ; then stuff it with all manner of sweet Herbs as you would ; then lay the Shoulder in the Caul, and sprinkle it with the Blood ; roast it, and make Venison-sauce, or Anchovies ; serve it.

107. *To Roast a Hare.*

Baste it with Cream as soon as it is laid down : But before you lay it down ; take a Marrow-bone, shred the Marrow with Salt, Nutmeg, Thyme, Savory, Parsly, Shalot, Onion chopt all small ; rowl them up in a good piece of Butter, and put it in the Belly of the Hare, and so roast it ; and after the first Basting with Cream, keep it constantly basted with Butter, till it's enough ; then take for Sauce a little Claret, a blade of Mace ;

dissolve

diffolve an Anchovy in it, and melt your
Butter very thick; then take the Pudding
out of the Belly, and wafh it all over with
the Butter; ferve it to the Table hot.

108. *A Neck or a Loin of Mutton in Cutlets.*

Firft cut all the Stakes out and hack them;
feafon with Salt, Pepper, Nutmeg, Parfly,
Thyme and Marjoram; chop them, and
ftrow them over with fome grated Bread;
wafh them over with drawn Butter, and lay
them on white Paper buttered, and made up
like a Dripping-pan, that it may not boil o-
ver; then boil them over Charcoal or Wood-
coal; and for Sauce, take Gravy, White-wine,
two Anchovies; mince a little Limon-peel,
with fome Orange very fmall; cut it into
Water, boil them up together, ftir in fome
Butter, fhake it up for Sauce; ferve it.

109. *A Neck or a Loin of Lamb fried.*

Cut every Rib afunder, beat them with
the back of a Knife; then fry them in about
a quarter of a Pint of Ale; ftrow on them
a little Salt, and cover them with a Plate
clofe; take them out with the Gravy in
them; fet them by the Fire, and have in
readinefs half a pint of White-wine, a few
Capers; fhred two Yolks of Eggs beat with
a little Nutmeg and Salt; wipe the Pan, and
put in the Sauce, and the Liquor they were
fried in; then ftir it with a Spoon all one
way

way until it be thick; then put in your Meat, ftir it all together; then difh it up with Limon and Parfly; ferve it.

110. *To Fry Beef.*

Take a piece of the Rump, cut it out into Stakes, beat them well with your Rowling-pin; then fry them in half a Pint of Ale; fprinkle them with Salt, an Onion cut fmall; and when it's fried enough, cut a little Thyme, Savory, Parfly and Shalot, with a little Onion and Nutmeg, then rowl up a piece of Butter in Flour, and fhake it up very thick; ferve it.

111. Take Beef-ftakes, of the Rib, half broil them; put them into your Stew-pan, cover them with Gravy; feafon them very high; rowl up a piece of Butter in Flour, and the Yolk of an Egg, and fend it.

112. And if in hafte, you may draw Gravy off an Oxe's Kidney; cut in two pieces, and feafoned high with Salt and Pepper: Put it into your Stew-pan, with Water enough to cover it; an Onion, a bunch of fweet Herbs, a piece of fweet Butter, draw the Gravy from it.

113. *Gravy to keep.*

Take a piece of coarfe Beef or Mutton, or what you have; cover it with Water, when

it

it has boiled a while take out the Meat;
beat it very well, and cut it into pieces to
let out the Gravy, with a bunch of sweet
Herbs, a little whole Pepper, an Onion;
some Salt; put it in again, let it stew but
not boil; and when you find it of a good
brown Colour, and it's enough; take it up
and put it into an Earthen-pot, so let it stand
to be cold; scum off all the Fat, and keep it
one Week under another; and if you find it
change, boil it up again, set it by for use;
and if for a brown Frigasee brown the Butter
in your Frying-pan, and shake in a little
Flour as it boils; put in the Gravy with a
Glass of Claret, shake up the Frigasee in it,
if for a white; then melt your Butter with a
spoonful or two of Cream, and the Yolks of
Eggs, White-wine or Syder.

114. *To make Gravy.*

Take a lean piece of Beef, cut and scotch
it in thin pieces, beat it well, and put in
a good piece of Butter in the Pan; fry it
brown till the Goodness is out, then throw
it away, and put into the Gravy a little Limon-peel, Cloves, Pepper and Salt, a Shalot
or two, a little large Mace, four Anchovies,
a Quart of strong Beef-broth, and half a Pint
of Claret, White-wine or Syder, as you
would have it, white or brown; boil it well
together, and when it's ready put it into an
Earthen-pot; set it by for use.

The

The Side-Diſhes.

115. *To Collar a Breaſt of Mutton.*

Take a large Breaſt of Mutton ; take off
the red Skin and all the Bones and Griſtles,
then grate White-bread, a little Cloves and
Mace, with the Yolk of three hard Eggs, a
little Limon-peel, ſweet Herbs and Chives
ſhred therein, and mix them with the Eggs,
Salt, Pepper, and all Spice ; make your Meat
lie flat and even ; then waſh and bone five
Anchovies, and lay up and down your Meat,
and ſtrow your Seaſoning over it ; then rowl
your Meat till like a Collar, and bind it
with coarſe Tape, and bake, boil or roaſt it ;
cut it into four pieces, and lay it in your
Diſh with ſtrong Gravy-ſauce, with Anchovies diſſolved in it, fried Oyſters and Force-
meat-balls : Garniſh with Limon and Barberries : A Side-diſh. But if for a Standing-
diſh ; then ſerve it with Cutlets in the Bottom, Sparrow-graſs, Colly-flowers Cabbage,
or what is in Seaſon, with white and black
Puddings, and Forc'd-meat-balls all about it.

116. *To make Olives.*

Take a Caul of a Breaſt of Veal, then lay a
Layer of Bacon, and take Chicken, Rabbets,
or Veal, with as much Marrow or Beef-
ſuet as Meat, with two Anchovies, Spinage,
Thyme, Marjoram, a few Chives, Limon-
peel, a little Salt, Pepper, Nutmeg, and beaten
Mace,

Mace, the Yolks of hard Eggs, a few Mushrooms and Oysters; beat all these in a Mor-
ter very fine, and lay a Layer of this and a
Layer of middling Bacon, and then rowl it
up hard in the Caul; then roast or bake it,
which you please; cut it into thin Slices,
and lay it in your Dish with strong Gravy-
sauce: A Side-dish.

117. *A Frigasee of Eggs.*

Take eight Eggs, boil them hard; cut
them into quarters into a Pint of strong
Gravy, and half a Pint of White-wine; season with Cloves and a blade of Mace, a little whole Pepper, a little Salt; scald a little Spinage to make them look Green, with
a Pint of large Oysters to lay round your
Dish; then put the Eggs in the Stew-pan,
with a few Mushrooms and Oysters, and
rowl up a piece of Butter in the Yolk of an
Egg and Flour, and shake it up thick for
Sauce, and you make Gravy-sauce, if you
please: Garnish with crispt Sippits, Limon
and Parsly: A Side-dish.

118. *Omulet of Eggs.*

Take what quantity of Eggs you please,
and beat them well; season them with Salt,
and whole Pepper, if you like it; then have
you Frying-pan ready with a good deal of
fresh Butter; let it be thoroughly hot; then
put in your Eggs with four spoonfuls of
strong

ſtrong Gravy; then have ready cut Parſly and Chives, and throw over 'em; and when it is enough turn it on the other ſide, and ſqueeze the Juice of a Limon, or an Orange over it; ſerve it: A Side-diſh.

119. *Petty Potatoes.*

Take a Pound of Butter, put it into a Stone-mortar, with half a pound of Naples-bisket, and half a pound of Jordan-Almonds, blanched and beaten; eight Eggs, with half the Whites; pound it all together till you don't know what it is, and put in ſome Sack and Orange-flower-water; ſweeten it to your Taſte with fine Sugar; then take a little fine Flour and make it into a ſtiff Paſte, and lay it on a Trencher, and have ready the quantity of two pound of Lard, and let it boil very faſt in your Frying-pan, and ſo cut the ſoft Paſte on the Trencher about the bigneſs of Cheſnuts, and throw them into the boiling Lard, and let them boil till they be yellow and brown, and when they are enough, take them up and drain the Fat from them in a Sieve, and put them into a Diſh, and pour for Sauce Sack and melted Butter; throw Double-refined Sugar: Then ſerve them for a Side-diſh.

120. *To make Toaſted Cheeſe.*

Take a pound of Cheſhire-Cheeſe, grate it fine into a Mortar; put in the Yolks of

two

two Eggs, and grate in a Penny Loaf; put in a quarter of pound of sweet Butter, so beat them all together, and then toast some white Bread very well, and spread upon your Toast; put them between two Dishes, with Fire underneath your Dish, and above: when they are brown serve them to the Table: A Side-dish. And these cannot be done but in a Dutch-stow.

121. *A Salamongundy.*

Take Chicken or Veal minced very fine; then lay a Layer of it, and a Layer of the Yolks of hard Eggs, and a Layer of the Whites; a Layer of Anchovies, a Layer of Limon; then a Layer of all sorts of Pickles, or as many as you have; and between every one of these lay a Layer of Sorrel, Spinage and Chives shred very fine, as the others; and when you have laid your Dish all round, that it's full, only leave a place a top to set an Orange or Limon: Garnish with Horse-radish, Limon and Barberries: This is proper for a second Course Side-dish, or a Middle-dish, for Supper: You must take two Dishes and lay the uppermost Dish to build the Salamongundy on, it being out of fashion to mix it all together, but every one mixes it on their Plates; some like it with the Juice of Limon, and some with Oil and Vinegar beat up thick together.

122. *To*

122. *To Pickle Pigeons.*

Take twelve Pigeons, bone half of them, and take off the Flesh of the other six, and beat them as fine as for Sausage-meat; mix it with Salt, Pepper, Spice and Herbs; a little Marrow, a little Limon-peel, three Anchovies, and the Yolks of hard Eggs, about two or three; then stuff the Pigeons full that you boned, the Herbs must be Sorrel, Spinage, young Betes, Vine-leaves, with a little Thyme, Marjoram and Savory; make your Pickle with Water, White-wine, and two Bay-leaves with a little Salt; boil the Bones in the Pickle, and when it's enough take them out, and set them to be cold; then put them in, to keep: A Side-dish. The same Way pickle Chickens when they are very young.

123. *Dutch Cheese.*

Take the quantity of three Pints of new Milk; beat seven Eggs very well, stir it in the new Milk, sweeten it with good Sugar very sweet; then put in a quarter of a pint of Sack, and a spoonful of Orange-flower-water, the same of Rose-water; set it over the Fire, and keep it stirring all the while till it comes to a tender Curd; put it in a Cloth, let the Whey run from it; then put it into Bisket-pans in what shape you please, lay it in your Dish: Then take some sweet
Cream,

Cream, and boil it with a Stick of Cinnamon, ſweeten it with fine Sugar, and beat the Yolks of two Eggs, and ſtir it in to thicken it ; keep it ſtirring all the Time that it may not raiſe a Skim, and when it's almoſt cold put in a ſpoonful of Sack, Orangeflower or Roſe-water; pour it over your Cheeſes when it's cold ; ſtick on the Cheeſes blanched Almonds cut in thin Slices : Serve it for a Side-diſh.

124. *Hedge-Hog.*

Take a pound of Jordan-Almonds, blanched and beaten in a Mortar very fine with a ſpoonful of Sack, or Orange-flower-water to keep them from Oiling ; make it into a ſtiff Paſte ; then beat in ſix Yolks and two Whites of Eggs, ſweeten it with fine Sugar with the quantity of half a Pint of Cream, and a quarter of a pound of ſweet Butter melted ; ſet it on your Stow, and keep it ſtirring till it's as ſtiff as you may make it into the Faſhion of a Hedge-hog ; then ſtick it full of blanched Almonds, ſlit and ſtick up like the Briſtles of a Hedge-hog ; then place it in the middle of your Diſh, and boil Cream, and take the Yolks of two Eggs, and ſweeten to your Taſte with Sugar; thicken it, but not too thick, pour it round your Hedge-hog, ſet it to be cold : Serve it for a Side-diſh.

125. *Black*

125. *Black Caps.*

Take the largeſt and beſt Pippins, cut them in Halves, don't pare them; take out their Cores, and put a little Limon-peel in their place: Lay them in a Mazarine-diſh with the Core-ſide downwards, and put in half a pint of Claret, a quarter of a pound of good Sugar; ſet them in the Oven with Tarts, and don't bake them too much; and when they are cold lay them in your Salver, with little Saucers of Caraway-comfits round them; pour the Liquor over them, and ſerve them for a Side-diſh.

126. *To Stew Pippins.*

Take the beſt Pippins, cut them into Halves, core them, and to three quarters their Weight put in Double-refined Sugar; put in as much Water as will cover them; then boil the Water and Sugar together; ſkim it well; cut in a little Limon-peel, and lay in your Pippins with their Core-ſide downwards; boil them up quick, and ſtew them till they look clear; then take them up and lay them in a Side-diſh, and ſtew the Liquor with a little White-wine, or the Juice of a Limon, or a little Cream, and the Yolk of an Egg or two, with a ſpoonful of Orange-flower-water, and pour it over them, inſtead of the Liquor; if you like that better: A Side-diſh.

F 2 127. *To*

127. *To Stew Pears.*

Take the greatest Warden-pears, bake them with brown Bread; put in a pint of strong Beer or Ale: When they are baked take them out of the Liquor; and take half a pint of it, and half a pint of Claret, and a quarter of a pound of Sugar; put them in the Stew-pan with two Cloves, a little Cream, cover them close, and let them stew till they are very red, turn them now and then; when they are enough put them into the Dish you intend to serve them to the Table in, with the Liquor they were stewed in; strow Double-refined Sugar over the Dish; Serve it for a Side-dish.

128. *Pippin Tansey.*

Take as many sliced Pippins as will cover the Pan's bottom; fry them with a soft Fire; then beat eight Eggs, whites and all, with a half-penny Loaf grated, and half a pint of Cream, a little Nutmeg and Sugar; then beat all these together, and pour over your fried Pippins; bake it over a soaking Fire; and when it's thoroughly baked on one side, turn it, and serve it with Butter melted thick, and Sugar round the brims of your Dish; A Side-dish.

129. *Goose-*

129. *Goosberry Tansey.*

Take a Quart of Green Goosberries, cut off the Tops and Tails, and boil them in half a pound of new Butter, in a Frying-pan, till they be well quodled; then pour into them the Yolks of fixteen Eggs, well beaten, with half a pint of Cream, and as much Sugar as will fweeten it to your Tafte; then boil it as you would a Tanfey, and when baked ftrow over it Rofe-water and Sugar; ferve it.

130. *Good Tanfey.*

Take twenty five Eggs, abating half the Whites; then beat them well with half a pint of Cream, or Milk, a pound of Naples-bisket grated very fine; then Colour it with a little Spinage, and a little Tanfey; fweeten it with Sugar, butter a Skillet and put in the Tanfey, ftirring it over the Fire continually; and when it boils to thicken pour it into your Pan; let your Butter be very hot before you put it in, fry it with the beft frefh Butter, keep a Plate over it, then turn it out, take care you don't break it in turning, then fqueeze in the Juice of an Orange over it, and ftrow Sugar on the Top, and round the brims of your Difh; ferve it.

F 3 131. *Almond*

131. *Almond Tansey*.

Take a pound of Almonds blanched, and
steep them in a pint of good Cream, ten Eggs,
four Whites; and when you have beat the
Almonds in a mortar, then put in the Sugar
with Crumbs of white Bread, then stir them
well together; fry them with fresh Butter, and
keep them stirring in the Pan till it's of a good
thickness; then strow over it fine Sugar, and
serve it.

132. *Dutch Wafers*.

Take a Quart of New Milk, or Cream;
warm it; then grate a Penny Loaf, or Bif-
ket, very fine, ten Eggs well beaten, with
a quarter of a pound of sweet Butter melted,
some Coriander-seeds, a little beaten Cloves,
a little Salt and fine Flour, enough to make
a Batter, like a Pan-cake, four spoonfuls of
Ale-yeast; mingle and stir them well together, and put them into an Earthen-pot; let
it stand covered with a Cloth before the
Fire, that it may warm and rise lightly near
the Fire three Hours; then let the Jorns be
made hot and clean, turned and buttered;
tye the Butter up in a fine Rag, and turn
them till both sides are hot over the Fire;
then put in the Batter, and bake the Wafers
well; don't burn them; and lay them warm
in a Dish; serve them very hot, with Sugar
grated over them, so eat them dry, or with
the

the Juice of a Limon, or an Orange; some put melted Butter and Sugar in the Dish, but they are best crispt and dry; serve them : A Side-dish.

133. *Court Fritters.*

Take a Pint of Sack; make a Posset with sweet Milk from the Cow; then take the Curd from the Posset and put it into a Bason, with six Eggs; season it with a little Nutmeg; beat it with a burchen Rod till you have beat it well together; then put Flour into it, and make it as Batter for Fritters: You may put in a little Sugar; then take clarified Beef-suet; make it boil before you put any in; serve it : A Side-dish.

134. *Skirret Fritters.*

Take a Pint of the Pulp of Skirrets, and a spoonful of fine Flour, the Yolks of Eggs with Sugar and Spice, make them into thick Batter; then fry them out into Fritters, and serve them with the rest of the Side-dishes, Madam.

135. *Little Puddings.*

Take a handful of grated Bread, a spoonful of Flour, the Yolks of two Eggs, a spoonful of Orange-flower-water, a handful of Beef-suet, shred all small, a little Nutmeg and Salt, a spoonful of Cheese-curds; work it well together, and wet it as little as you

can,

can and make it up with Cream, or new
Milk, lay it in round Balls in the bottom
of your Diſh, which muſt be well buttered ;
bake them not too much; when they are
baked put them in another Diſh, with a
ſpoonful of Sack or White-wine, melted
Butter and Sugar together poured on them ;
ſerve them.

136. *Sweat-bread Paſties.*

Take Sweat-breads, parboil them, ſhred
them very fine ; then put to them Marrow,
or the Fat of a Loin of Veal ſhred, with a
little grated Bread, and the Yolks of two
Eggs, a little Cream, Roſe-water, Sugar,
and grated Nutmeg; temper all theſe together ; then make Puff-paſte with Butter
rowled in the Flour, with a little Sugar and
Roſe-water, the Yolks of two Eggs, and
cold Water ; then rowl it out like little Pa-
ſties the breadth of your Hand, and put
your Meat in them, and fry them brown,
or bake them ; ſerve them.

137. *Kidney Paſties.*

Take the Kidney of a Loin of Veal, with
the Fat about it, with a little of the cold Veal
you have dreſs'd, then take Marrow, or Beef-
ſuet, with the Yolks of Eggs, and chop them
all very fine together, pound a little Cloves,
Mace, Nutmeg, and a little Spice, Salt, Limon-peel, and what quantity of Sugar and
Cur-

Currans you think fit: Mix them well together, and make little Pasties of Puff-paste,
and fry them in Hog's-lard to make them
look brown and yellow.

138. *Paste to Fry.*

Take grated Bread and Curds, and two
Whites of Eggs, and make it almost as thick
as Paste; wet it with a little Cream, and
make it into what Fashion you please; fry
them in Butter as you did your Puddings:
Make for Sauce, Butter, Sugar, Rose-water,
and Sack well beaten together; pour it upon them; send it.

139. *Cheese Loaves.*

Take Cheese-curd, grated Bread, Yolks of
Eggs, Mace, Nutmeg, mix them well together, and sweeten it to your Taste with Sugar; then take some Stone-porringers, butter them, and put in the Curd; bake them,
but not too much: When they are baked
turn them out, and cut a little hole in the
Tops, and put Butter in them; set them in
the Oven again to rise, and Colour them;
serve them.

140. *Pippin Tarts.*

Take two small Oranges, pare them thin,
and boil them in Water till they be tender;
then shred them small, and pare twenty Pippins; quarter and core them, and put to
them

them ſo much Water as will boil them till
they are enough; then put in half a pound
of white Sugar, and take the Orange-peel
that is ſhred, and the Juice of the Oranges,
and let them boil till they are pretty thick;
then ſet them by to cool; make open Tarts,
and put it in; ſet them in the Oven mode-
rate hot: Set them by for uſe.

141. *To Stew Pippins.*

Take a Gallon of the beſt Pippins, pare
and quarter them; cut out the Cores and
ſtew them in a little Sack, and Roſe-water;
ſeaſon them with a little beaten Cinnamon,
Nutmeg and Sugar, and ſqueeze in a Limon;
let them ſtew till they are very tender; and
when they are cold uſe them for Taffata-
tarts, Madam.

142. *Orange-tarts.*

Take *Sevile* Oranges, grate a little of the
out-ſide Rinds; ſlit them in Halves, and
ſqueeze out the Juice into a China-diſh, and
throw the Peel into Water, change it three
times a Day, for two Days; then have ready a skillet of Water; which muſt boil before you put your Oranges in: You muſt
boil them in two Waters to take the Bitter-
neſs away: When they are tender take them
out and dry them in a Cloth; then beat it
in a Stone-mortar till it's very fine; then
take their Weight in refined Sugar, and boil
it

it to a Syrup, and skim it clean before you put in your Pulp; then boil it all together till it looks clear, and when it's ready let it stand till it's cold, and then have ready some Puff-paste in Patty-pans, and put your Oranges in; and juft before you put them in the Oven, make a Hole on the Top of your Tarts, and put in the Juice and bake them in a quick Oven.

143. *Bean-tarts.*

Take Green Beans, boil them, and blanch them, then make Puff paste, and put into Patty-pans; then put a Layer of Beans, and a Layer of all forts of wet Sweet-meats, except Quinces; ftrow in a little Sugar between every Layer; then cover your Tarts, and make a Hole on the Top, and put in a quarter of a Pint of the Juice of Limon: Put in Marrow feafoned with Cloves, Mace, Nutmeg and Salt, candied Limon and Orange-peel; and when they come out of the Oven, put into ever Tart fome White-wine, thickned up with the Yolk of an Egg, and a bit of Butter; and thefe Tarts are to be eat hot.

144. *Spinage-Tarts.*

Take Marrow, Spinage, hard Eggs, of each a Handful, Cloves, Mace, Nutmeg, Limon-peel fhred very fine; then put in as many Currans as you think fit, with Raifins ftoned,

ftoned, and fhred, candied Orange and Citron-peel; fweeten it to your Tafte; make Puff-pafte, and make them into little fquare Pafties; bake or fry them.

145. *Tart de Moy.*

Make Puff-pafte and lay round your Difh; then lay a Layer of Bisket, and a Layer of Butter aud Marrow, and then a Layer of all forts of wet Sweet-meats, or as many as you have, and fo do till the Difh is full; then boil a Quart of Cream, and thicken it with fou. Eggs, and a fpoonful of Orange-flower-water, fweeten it with Sugar, and half an Hour will bake it.

146. *Set Cuftards.*

Take a Quart of Cream, fet it on the Fire; boil it with fome broad Mace; when it's boiled fet it to be cold; then take fix Eggs, with half the Whites; beat them very well, and put in a fpoonful of Orange-flower-water, or Rofe-water, and put in a pound of Sugar; harden the Cruft in the Oven, and ftuff the Corners with brown Paper, and prick the bottom with a fmall Pin, when you fet them, and fill them; and when they are enough fet them by for ufe.

147. *To make Cuftards.*

Take a quart of Cream, boil it with a blade of Mace; beat ten Eggs, leave out half the
Whites;

Whites; take the Mace out, and sweeten it
with Sugar; then beat in the Eggs with one
spoonful of Sack, one spoonful of Orange-
flower-water; sweeten it to your Taste, and
put it into your Custard-cups, and let them
but just boil up in the Oven; and if you
boil the Eggs in the Cream all together, then
you may put it in your Custard cups, over
Night, and they will be fit for use.

148. *Rice Custards.*

Take a Quart of Cream, boil it with a
blade of Mace; then put to it boiled Rice,
well beaten with your Cream; put them together, and stir them well all the while it
boils on the Fire; and when it's enough take
it off, and sweeten it to your Taste, and put
in a little Rose-water; let them be cold,
then serve them.

149. *Cheese-Cakes.*

Take a Quart of Cream, boil it; then beat
the Yolks of two Eggs; and when the Cream
is cold put in the Eggs, and put it on again,
and boil it till it comes to a Curd, but not
to Whey; then blanch Almonds, beat them
with Orange-flower-water, and put 'em into the Cream with a little Naples-bisket, and
a little Green Citron, shred small, with Musk-
plumbs ground in the Sugar; sweeten it to
your Taste with good Sugar; rowl it out
thin, and bake them, but let not your Oven
be too hot.   150. *Cheese-*

150. *Cheese-Cakes, another Way.*

Take two Gallons of New Milk, turn it
with Runnet, that it may be a tender Curd;
and when it's come and gathered, run it
through a thin Strainer, and press out the
Whey very dry; then beat the Curd with a
pound of sweet Butter very well; then put
to it twelve Eggs, with the Whites of six;
season it with Cloves, Mace, Cinnamon,
Nutmeg and Ginger, a little Salt and Rose-
water, and what quantity of Currans you
please, season it to your Taste with Sugar,
with a Musk-plumb or two ground in it:
Then bake them for Use.

151. *For the Paste.*

Take fine Flour, break in two Eggs, with
three spoonfuls of Orange-flower, or Rose-
water, and fair Water mixed together, as
much as will make it into a stiff Paste; then
rowl it out thin, and put in the rest of the
Butter; then make your Crust, and half an
Hour will bake them; and you may venture to eat them.

To Pot and Collar.

152. *To Pot Salmon.*

Take what piece you have; season it
with Cloves, Mace, a little Salt and Pepper, two Bay-leaves: Put it into a Pot
with

with as much melted Butter as will cover
it; then set it in the Oven with Manchet-
Bread; and when it's baked take it out
of the Pot, and put it into the Pot you
intend to keep it in, and pour the Butter off, and clarifie it, and cover it very
well; and if you find it's not seasoned
high enough, season it higher; then put
it into the other Pot; and the same
Way pot Trouts or Eels, only you must
bone them.

153. *To Pot Tongues.*

Take Neat's-Tongues out of the Pickle,
when they have lain long enough to look
red, cut off the Roots and boil them till
they will Peel; then take your Tongues
and season them with Salt, Pepper, Cloves,
Mace and Nutmeg: Rub it into them well
with your Hands when they be hot; then
put 'em into a Pot, and melt as much Butter
as will cover them, and put them into the
Oven and bake them; and when they are
baked take them out of the Pot, and put
them into the Pot you intend to keep
them in; pour off all the Butter, and keep
back the Gravy, and melt as much more
as will cover it an Inch above your Tongues, and you may fill up the Sides of the
Pot, with Chickens or Pigeons

150. *To*

154. To Pot Lobsters.

Boil the Lobsters till they will come out of their Shells; then take these, Tails and Claws, and season them with Mace, Salt and Pepper; then put them into a Pot and bake them with sweet Butter; and when they come out of the Oven, take them out of the Pot, and put them into a long Pot, and clarify the Butter they were baked in, with as much more as will cover them very well; set them by for use.

155. To Pot Beef like Venison.

Cut a large veiny piece of Beef into four pieces; skin it and beat it with your Rowling-pin; then take two penny-worth of Salt-petre, the same of Sal-prunellæ; beat it very fine, and rub it well in with your Hands; lay it in a Tray for two Days; turn it once a Day, then take it out; season it with Salt and Pepper pretty high; then cut a little Beef suet into long slices; season it with Salt and Pepper, and lay it in your Pot, then the Beef, and a Top break into small pieces two pound of fresh Butter, tye it down and bake it with brown Bread; when it's bak'd take it out of the Pot with a skimmer, to drain the Gravy from it, and put it into a Mortar, and take out all the Skins and Veins, and beat it with a little of the Butter that you must skim off; then put it into

another

another Pot, and pour the Butter over it, keep back the Gravy; and if there is not Butter enough to cover it, clarifie as much as will cover it an Inch above the Meat; let it stand four Days in your Cellar before you cut it to eat; the same Way Pot Venison, only you must not beat it in a Mortar, and use black Pepper instead of white.

156. *To Pot Pork.*

Take a Leg, or any fleshy piece of Pork, skin it, and cut it out in pieces; beat it in a Mortar very fine; season it high with Salt and Pepper; shred a good handful of Sage, a handful of Rosemary; mix it together, and put it into a Pot to bake, with a pound of Butter, bake it with brown Bread, and when it comes out of the Oven, take it out with care, and drain it from the Gravy; then put it into a dry Pot, and press it down close and hard; skim off all the Butter, and put to it, and clarifie as much more as will cover an Inch above the Meat: Then wet Paper, cover it and set it in your Cellar: In four Days cut it.

157. *To make Sausages.*

Take a Loin of Pork, skin and bone it; then break the bones all to pieces, put them into Water enough to cover them, when they boil skim them clean, then season the Liquor with Salt, Pepper, a blade of Mace, Shalot, Onion,

G

Onion; and when all the Goodness is out of the Bones, take it out and strain it, and let it be cold, then shred your Meat very fine, season it with Salt, Pepper, beaten Cloves and Mace, a handful of Sage, a little Rosemary, a handful of Spinage to make them look Green; then mix them together with the Yolks of three Eggs, with as much of the Liquor as will make it pretty moist, then rowl up one of them in flour, and fry it, to see if its seasoned to your Mind; if not, season as you like them; and if they are not to keep, shred in a few Oysters with their Liquor, and fill them.

158. *To Pot Fowls.*

Pick them clean, and singe them with white Paper: Dry them with a Cloth; don't wash them; if you do, they won't keep; then season them with Salt, Pepper, Cloves, Mace and Nutmeg, beaten and mix all together: Let them stand twenty-four Hours; then place them in the Pot, with their Breasts downwards: strow over them some whole Cloves and Mace; then pour as much melted Butter as will cover them; tye them down close, and bake them; and when they are baked enough, let them stand a little, and then drain the Gravy from them; then place them in another Pot, with their Breasts upwards; fill their Craws with Butter, pour off all the Top of the Butter,

keep

keep back the Gravy, and the things in the bottom, and let your Butter be an Inch above your Fowls, fix Ducks will endure two Hours baking, and other Fowls, more or less, according to their bigness; then set them in your Cellar for use.

160. *To Pot Pigeons.*

Pick them very clean, wipe them with a clean Cloth, don't wash them; season them with Salt and Pepper; rowl up a piece of Butter in the Seasoning, and put in their Bellies; fix Pigeons will take up a pound of Butter; place them in the Pot, with their Breasts downwards; dridge 'em with Flour before you put them in, and tye them down close; and when they are baked take them out, and put them in another Pot, with their Breasts upwards, keep back the Gravy; and if you have not Butter enough, clarifie as much as will cover them; set them in your Cellar.

160. *To Pot Hares.*

Take a Hare, wash him clean, dry him well from the Blood, with a Cloth; cut him into quarters; season him with Salt, Pepper, Cloves, Mace and Nutmeg: Put it in a Pot with a pound of Butter, and two Bay-leaves, and when it comes out of the Oven take out the Bones, and put it in a Mortar, and beat it fine, and pour the Butter from the Gravy,

G 2   and

and mix it all together with your Hands, and put it into a glazed Venison-pot, that you intend to serve it to the Table in; press it down close, and clarifie as much Butter as will cover it an Inch above your Meat; set it by for Use.

161. *To Collar Beef.*

Take a large Flank of Beef, beat it with your Rowling-pin to make it lie flat, and even; cut it smooth, and take out all the Gristles and Veins; then take one Ounce of Salt-petre, the same of Sal-prunellæ; beat it small, and take a quarter of a pound of brown Sugar: Mix them together, and rub it in well with your Hands; then lay it in a Tray, and sprinkle it once a Day with Pump-water; let it lie three Days; then season it with Salt, Pepper, Nutmeg, and all sorts of sweet Herbs, a good deal of Sage, one Sprig of Rosemary; cut them, and throw it over the Collar; then rowl it up hard and close like a Collar of Brawn, and bind it about with coarse Tape very tight, and put it into Water enough to cover it; season it with Salt, Pepper, and a little whole Mace, a bundle of sweet Herbs, two Bay-leaves, an Onion; and when it's baked, rowl it up hard in a coarse Cloth, and let it lie till next Day, and then you may eat it if you please: Or, you may keep it in the Liquor it was baked in; when it's cold take off

the

the Fat, and boil it with more Water; and if it's not seasoned high enough, season it higher; set it to be cold; then put your Beef into a long Pot, and cover it with the Pickle; and if you keep it a pretty while, boil up the Pickle as you find occasion.

162. *To Collar a Breast of Veal.*

Take a large Breast of Veal; bone it, and take out all the Gristles; then take Sage, Thyme, Marjoram, Savory, Chives, a little Limon-peel; shred them small, and mix them with Salt, Pepper, Nutmeg, three hard Eggs, hacked small; cut your Meat to make it lie flat, and even; bone five Anchovies with four Ounces of Bacon; slice it thin, and lay with the Anchovies up and down your Meat, and strow your Seasoning and Herbs upon it, and shred some Marrow and Beef-suet together, and mix with the other Ingredients, and rowl it up hard, and tye it with coarse Tape, and cut it into three Collars; tye them severally in clean Cloths very tight and hard at both Ends; then make your Pickle as follows:

Your Pickle thus:

Set on a Pot with half Milk and Water, and put in the Veal-bones, with a bunch of sweet Herbs, Mace, Nutmeg, Salt and whole Pepper, and a Bay-leaf; when all these are boiled well, till all the Goodness

G 3

is out, take out the Bones, and put in the
Collars, and let them boil tender; then take
them out and tye them up hard in clean
Clothes, and hang them up till they are
cold; then skim off all the Fat of the Pickle,
and when they are boiled enough, and the
Broth cold, put them in and boil up the
Pickle, as you find occasion; eat it with
Oil and Vinegar beat up thick together, or
the Juice of a Limon, and Pickles as you
please.

163. To Collar a Pig.

Take a fat Pig, cut off his Head, and
chine him down the Back, and take out all
the Bones and Gristles; take care you don't
cut the Skin; then lay it in Spring-water
one Night, the next Morning dry it in a
Cloth, and cut each side asunder; season it
with Salt, whole Pepper, Nutmeg, and a
little beaten Mace, a little Sage, Rosemary,
and Limon-peel; rowl them up hard in a
Cloth, and the sousen Drink is Bran, Milk
and Water; strain out the Bran, and skim
off all the Fat, and let your Collars be cold
before you put them in.

164. To Callar Eels.

Skin them and rip up their Bellies, and
take out their Guts and Bones; then season
them with Salt, Pepper, Nutmeg, Limon-
peel and sweet Herbs, and rowl them up
hard

hard in coarse Tape; then put on a Pot of
Water, so make your Pickle, and put in the
Bones of your Eels, with Salt, Pepper, and
a bunch of Herbs, three Bay-leaves, a sprig
of Rosemary, and boil them, but not too
much; boil some Syder in the Pickle; and
when you take them up tye them close, and
hang them up to be cold; and when the
Liquor is cold, skim off all the Fat, and put
in the Collars; boil up the Pickle now and
then, as you find occasion, and eat it with
Oil and Vinegar beat up thick together, or
the Juice of Limon, Pickles, or what you
please.

THE PICKLES.

165. *To Pickle Milons, or great* cucumbers

Take the largest and greenest Cucumbers;
cut a piece in their sides the length of your
Cucumbers, take out their Seeds and drain
them well; then put into them some Cloves,
Mace, whole Pepper and Mustard-seed bruised a little; then peel three Cloves of Garlick, the same of Shalot, with some Ginger
sliced thin, according to the quantity; and
put in a little Salt; then lay the piece on
again that you cut out, and tye it fast and
close with Packthread; then put them into
as much White-wine Vinegar as will cover
them very well; and put in a good deal of
made Mustard, and a Bay-leaf, with Salt,

G 4 according

according to the quantity you make; let
them lie in the cold Pickle nine Days; Then
put them in a Braſs-Kettle, and ſet them
over the Fire to Green; ſtove them down
cloſe, and let them have a boil or two; then
take them off and ſtove them down very
cloſe, and let them ſtand to Green; then ſet
them on again, and ſo do till they are very
Green; then take them out, and boil up the
Pickle, and pour it over them ſcalding-hot;
then cover your Pot, and tye it down cloſe
with Leather: You may eat them next Day,
or you may keep them a Year.

166. *To Pickle Wall-nuts.*

Take Wall-nuts when you can juſt thruſt
a Pin through them; then make a Pot of
Water boil; take it off, let it cool a little;
then put in your Wall-nuts, let them lie ſeven Days; then make a Pot of Water boil,
and put them in; let them boil a quarter of
an Hour; then wipe them dry, and put them
into as much White-wine Vinegar as will
cover them two Inches above the Nuts; then
put in Cloves, Mace, Nutmeg and Ginger,
whole white Pepper, Muſtard-ſeed bruiſed,
ſeven Cloves of Garlick, the ſame of Shalot,
according to the quantity you make, all peeled; a Nutmeg cut into quarters; put all
theſe together, and let them ſtand in the
cold Pickle nine Days; then pour the Pickle
from them; boil it up and ſet it by to be
cold;

cold; then put in your Nuts, and tye them down close with Leather: Set them by for Use.

167. *To Pickle French beans.*

Take French-beans when they are very young, Top and Tail them; put them into the best White-wine Vinegar, with Salt, and a little whole Pepper, a Race of Ginger, cut grofs; let them lie in the cold Pickle nine Days; then boil your Pickle in a Brafs Kettle, and put your Beans in, let them but just have a boil; then take them off the Fire, stove them down close, set them by; then put them on again; so do six times, till they are as Green as Grafs; then put them into an Earthen-pot; tye it down close with Leather, and they will keep all the Year. The same Way you may do Cucumbers, Purfly-stalks; and if they do change Colour, boil up the Pickle and pour over them scalding-hot.

168. *To Pickle Colly-flowers.*

Take the whiteft and clofeft Colly-flowers; cut them the length of your Finger from the Stalks; then boil them in a Cloth, with half Milk and Water, don't boil them tender; then take them out carefully, and set them by to be cold; then take the best White-wine Vinegar, Cloves, Mace and Nutmeg, cut into quarters; a little whole white
Pepper,

Pepper, and a Bay-leaf; so let these boil
well in the Vinegar, and set them to be cold;
then put in your Colly-flowers, and in three
Days they will be fit to eat. The same way
pickle white Cabbage-Stalks, young Turneps; pare them pretty thick, and cut them
the bigness of Mushrooms.

169. To Pickle Plumb-buds.

Take Salt and Water, boil it together;
then put in your Plumb-buds, and boil them
not tender, then strain them from the Water, and let them be cold; then take what
quantity you think fit of White-wine Vinegar, and boil it with two blades of Mace,
and a little whole Pepper, then put them into the Pickle, and let them stand nine Days,
then scald them in a brass Kettle, six times,
till they are as green as Grass; take care
they are not soft; tye them down with Leather: The same way pickle Elder-buds, and
they are very pretty.

170. To Pickle Mushrooms.

Take the Button Mushrooms, wipe them
clean with a piece of Flannel, and throw
them into half Milk, and half Water, then
set on your Preserving-pan, with half Milk
and Water, and when it boils put in your
Mushrooms, and let them boil up quick for
half a quarter of an Hour, then pour them
into a Sieve, let them drain till they be
cold;

cold; then make your Pickle of the beſt White-wine Vinegar, put in Mace, Long-pepper; a Race of Ginger boiled in it, and when it's enough, cut a Mutmeg into quar-ters, and put in it, and let it ſtand till it's cold, then put it into a Glaſs, and pour a little of the beſt ſweet Oil you can get to preſerve them, tye it down with Leather; ſet it by for Uſe.

Another excellent Way to Pickle Muſhrooms.

Put your Muſhrooms into Water, and waſh them with a Spunge, (put them in Water as you do them) then put Water and a little Salt, when it boils put in your Muſhrooms, and when they boil up ſkim them clean, and put them into cold Water, and a little Salt, let them ſtand twenty-four Hours, and put the Water from them, and put them into White-wine Vinegar, and let them ſtand a Week; then take your Pickle from them, and boil it very well, put ſome whole Pepper, Cloves, Mace, and a little all Spice; when your Pickle is cold, put it to the Muſhrooms, and keep them cloſe ſtopt, or tyed with a Bladder to keep the Air from them, or elſe they will be apt to mother; if they do mother, you muſt boil your Pickle a-gain: If you pleaſe you may make your Pickle half White-wine.

To

171. *To Pickle Asparagus.*

Take a hundred of the largest Asparagus, cut off the White at the Ends, and scrape them lightly to the Head, till they look green, wipe them with a Cloth, lay 'em in a broad Gally-pot, very even, throw over them two-penny-worth of whole Cloves and Mace, a little Salt, put in as much White-wine Vinegar as will cover them well, for all Pickles do waste in standing: Let them lie in the cold Pickle nine Days, then pour the Pickle out into a Brass-Kettle, and let it boil, then put it in, and stove them down very close, set them by a little, then set them over again till they are very green, take care they don't boil to be soft, then put them in a large Gally-pot, place them even; tye them down with Leather.

172. *To Pickle Samphire.*

Take Samphire, and pick it, and lay it into Salt and Water for two Days, then take it out and put it into a Brass-pot, and cover it with the best White-wine Vinegar very well, for it will waste mightily, having it over a slow Fire; cover it very close, let it hang till it's very green, and crisp, but not tender nor soft, then put it up, and tye it down close with Leather: The best time to do this in, is the Month of *May*; then it's in high Season.

173. *To*

173. *To Pickle Barberries.*

Take Barberries, piek out fome of the worſt to make the Pickle look red; put in Bay-ſalt, and White-ſalt, to make it ſtrong enough to bear an Egg; then ſtrain the Liquor into the Pot you intend to keep them in; and when the Liquor is cold, put in the Barberries, with as much White-wine Vinegar as you think fit, with half a pound of brown Sugar, tye them down cloſe with Leather; ſet them by for Uſe.

174. *To keep Artichoke-bottoms.*

Take Artichokes and throw them into Salt and Water for half a Day; then make a Pot of Water boil, and put in your Artichokes, and let them boil till you can juſt draw the Leaves from the Bottoms; then cut out the Bottoms very handſome, and ſmooth; then put them into a Pot with Salt, Pepper and Vinegar, a few Cloves, two Bay-leaves; then pour ſome melted Butter over them, enough to cover them, then tye it down cloſe for Uſe: Then put them into boiling Water, with a piece of Butter in the Water, to plump them; then uſe them as you pleaſe.

175. *To dry Artichoke-bottoms.*

Order them as the others; only inſtead of putting them into Pickles, lay 'em on Sieves, and

and set them in an Oven after Houshold-
bread is drawn; so dry them well: When
you use them put them into boiling Water,
with a piece Butter to plump them.

176. To keep Green Pease.

Take young Pease, shell them, and put
them in the Pot when it boils; let them
have two or three boils; then spread a
Cloth on your Table, and dry them very
well in it; then have your Bottles ready
dried, and fill them to the Necks, and pour
over them melted Mutton-Fat, and cork
them down very close, that no Air can
come to them; set them in your Cellar;
and when you use them put them into boiling Water, with a spoonful of good Sugar,
a good piece of Butter; and when they are
enough drain them and shake them up
thick; at *Christmas* you may venture to eat
them.

177. To keep Goosberries.

Take the largest *Dutch* Goosberries at full
growth; before they change Colour; top
and tail them, don't cut them too close;
then put them into wide-mouthed Glass-
bottles, which must be very dry; stop them
down, and put them into a Kettle of cold
Water; let it heat leisurely; and when you
think the Goosberries are scalded thoroughly, take them out; and when they are cold,
knock

knock in the Corks, and seal them down clofe, that they take no Air: Then make Ufe of them for Tarts, or what you pleafe.

178. *Damfons* are done the fame Way, only you muſt put them into Stone-Bottles; and if you put them into a great Pot, cover them over with clarified Mutton-Fat; fet them by for Ufe.

179. *To Pickle Cucumbers.*

Firſt waſh your Cucumbers; then put them into a Rundlet with one End, and head it up clofe : Take Water and Salt and ſtir it together, till it will bear an Egg; then boil it and skim it very well, and put it into your Veffel boiling-hot, and fo let it ſtand three Weeks : Then open the Head of your Veffel, and take out the Cucumbers clean from the Water, and put them into another Veffel. 'At the Bottom whereof lay fome Dill, Fennel, and *Jamaica*-Pepper, and a little Allom, which will make them crifp; and ftrow fome of thefe Ingredients among them; then head up your Veffel again; put in boiling Vinegar, and let them ſtand a Week : And if you find they are not Green enough, you muſt boil the Vinegar again; put it to 'em and ſtop your Veffel clofe.

180. *A*

180. *A very good Sauce for roaft Venifon.*

Take one Glafs of Claret, one Glafs of
fair Water, one Glafs of Vinegar, one large
Onion ftuck full of Cloves, one Spoonful
of whole Pepper, one of beaten Pepper, and
one of Salt; boil all together with fome
Anchóvies; ftrain the Liquor through a
Sieve, and ferve it up with the Venifon.

Bills of FARE,

Proper for moſt Months in the Year.

JANUARY.

1.
Raw-fiſh Soop.
Mutton forced.
Boiled Geeſe.
Hanch of Veniſon roaſt.
Frigaſee of Rabbets.

2.
Capons roaſt.
Kidney-beans.
Hanch of Veniſon roaſt.
Frigaſee of Rabbets.
Butter'd Crabs.

1.
Geeſe Alamode.
Boiled Mutton with
Colly-flowers.
Pigeon-Pye.
Roaſt Lamb.
Pork Roaſt.

2.
Rabbets roaſt.
Peaſe.
Stewed Pippins.
Potted Veniſon.
Skirret Fritters.

FEBRUARY.

1.
Scotch Collops.
Lamb roaſt.
Egg-pye.
Mutton boiled.

Bacon Froiſe.
2.
Green-Geeſe.
Rasberry-Cream.
Rabbets roaſt.
Collar'd

Collar'd-Beef, or Veal.
Cold Ham.

    1.

Jibblets stewed.
Veal Collops.
Mutton roast.
Rice-pudding.
Beef boiled.

    2.

Chickens and Rabbets
   roast.
Goosberry Tarts.
Pease.
Strawberries and Cream
Cold Salmon.

    3.

Pigeons and Bacon.
White Frigasee of Chic-
   ken.
Lamb roast.
Dish of boil'd Puddings.
Boiled Pork.

    2.

Ducks roast.
Apple-pye and Cream.
Asparagus.
Chicken-pye.
Sturgeon.

    1.

Geese Alamode.
Mutton boiled.
Lamb-pye.
Veal roast.
Jibblets stewed.

    2.

Three Chickens three
   Rabbets roast.
Pease.
Codling-tart and Cream
Cold Tongues.
Salmon boiled and pic-
   kled.

    1.

Brown Soop.
Large Dish of Fish.
Ragow of Veal.
Bread Pudding.
Leg of Mutton roast.

    2.

Eels spickcockt with
   Smelts.
Shourdens.
Herrings and Toasts.
Sturgeon.
Butter'd Apple-pye.

MARCH.

    1.

Asparagus Soop.

Boiled Veal and Bacon.
Apple-pudding.

       Lamb

Lamb roaſt.
2.
Pigeons ſoaſt.
Omlet of Eggs.
Oyſters in Shells.
Spinage paſty.
1.
Griskins of Beef.
Hogs-puddings.
Lamb in Joints.
2.
Rabbets and Chicken.
Salamongundy.
Shred Veniſon.

Lamb - ſtones, Sweet-breads, Artichoke-bottoms ragowed.
1.
Turkeys and Marrow-bones.
Chicken frigaſeed.
Stake-pye.
Veal roaſt.
2.
Roaſt Lamb.
Peaſe.
Wafers.
Tarts.

MAY, JUNE and JULY.

1.
Boiled Veal and Bacon.
Lamb frigaſeed.
Mutton roaſt.
Chicken-pye,
Beef boiled.
2.
Rabbets roaſt.
Chine of Salmon.
Goosberry-fool.
Tarts.
Cold Tongues.
1.
Peaſe-ſoop.
Leg of Mutton and Colly-flowers.

Veal Cutlets.
Beef roaſt.
Carrot-pudding.
2.
Ducks roaſt.
Artichokes.
Chicken roaſt.
Cheeſe-cakes.
Collar'd-Beef or Pig.
1.
Beef Royal.
Pigeons and Bacon.
Lamb-pye.
Roaſt Veal.
Italian-pudding.

H 2   2. *Partridges*

2.

Partridges roaſt.
Kidney-beans.
Craw-fiſh in Jelly.
Pig's Petty-toes.
Collar'd-Beef.

1.

A Pottage.
Mutton boiled.
Fruit-pudding.
Phillet of Veal roaſt.

2.

Green-Geeſe roaſt.
Peaſe.
Goosberry-Tart.
Cold Tongues.

1.

Pike dreſt with Oyſters.
Bread-pudding.
Mutton Cutlets.
Shoulder of Veal ſtufft.

2.

Wild Pigeons.
Petty Portoons.
Pullets forced.
Apple-pye.

1.

Pullets Pellone.
Limon-pudding　with
　Pan-cakes.
Collops half larded.
Mutton in Cutlets.

2.

Lamb in Joints.
Peaſe.
Salmon or Gudins.
Tanſey with Fritters.

1.

Pullets Alamode.
Carrot-pudding.
Lamb-pye ſweet.
Mutton roaſt.

2.

Turkeys with Eggs.
Morrels & Artichokes.
Collar'd Pig.
Almond-Tarts.

1.

Boiled Beef.
Veal Cutlets.
Mutton roaſt.
Fruit-pudding.

2.

Ducks roaſt.
Peaſe.
Tongues.
Cold Sallets.

1.

Pike roaſt.
Mutton boiled.
Potato pye.
A Phillet of Veal ſtufft.

2.

Chicken roaſt.
　　　　　　Tanſey.

Tanfey.
Oyfters in Shells.
Potted Eels.

1.

Pottage with Rice.
Almond-pudding.
Green-fifh with Eggs.
Mutton roaft.

2.

Turkeys ftufft and lard-
ed.
Roaft Sweet-breads.
Collar'd Pig.
Tart De-moy.

1.

Beef Alamode.
Lamb frigafeed.

Pootage A-la-Rein.
Partridge-pye.
Pottage Sante.

Fifh.
Fifh.

Pigeons marrownate.
Turkey dob'd.
Veal Cutlets ragou'd.
Marrow-pudding.

To remove.
Venifon roaft.

Neck of Veal in Cut-
lets.
Mutton roaft.

2.

Rabbets roaft.
Collar'd-beef.
Eggs in Gravy.

1.

Peafe-foop.
Salt-fifh with Eggs.
Breaft of Veal collar'd.
Pigeon-pye.

2.

Green Geefe.
Pan-cakes.
Parfnips buttered.
Sturgeon.

AUGUST.

Chine of Mutton and
Collops.

Second Courfe

Fowl.
Peach-fritters.
Mufhrooms.
Tarts.
Morrels.
Salamongundy.
Fowl.

Soals.
Craw-fifh.

Oyfters

| Oyster-loaves. | Artichokes. |
| Sweet-breads. | French-beans. |

SEPTEMBER.

1.

A Pottage.
Boiled Fish.
An Olive-pudding.
Mutton roast.

2.

Roast Chicken.
Scarrots boiled.
Tart De-Moy.
Calf's Liver larded.

1.

Calf's-head hashed.
Salmon boiled.
Lamb in Joints.
Marrow-pudding.

2.

Roast Geese.
Almond-puffs.
Rabbets roast.
Asparagus.

1.

Bacon and Chicken.
Lamb frigaseed with
    Artichokes.
Petty of Sweet-breads
    and Livers.
Mutton roast.

2.

Woodcocks with Toasts.
Marrow-pudding.
Spinage-tarts.
Forced Trouts.

1.

Lamb with Spinage
    and Goosberries.
Bread-pudding.
Griskins of Beef.
Shoulder of Mutton.

2.

Pullets with Eggs.
Lapires.
Potted Partridges.
Almond-Tarts.

1.

Chicken and Rabbets
    roast, a Calf's-head
    hashed.
Asparagus.
Potted Eels.
Cheese-cakes.

2.

Beef Lorreine.
Turkeys boiled, with
    Tarts.

Petty

Petty Partoons.
Mutton Cutlets.

1.

Two Pullets stuft with
  Oysters.
Lamb in Joints.
Clary in Cakes.
Trotter-pye.

2.

Calf's-head hashed.
Petty of Pigeons.
Mutton Collops broil-
  ed, or a Pig.
Roast-beef: This is to
  be before the Chic-
  ken and Rabbets.

OCTOBER.

1.

Cod's-head boiled.
Mutton boiled.
Pigeon-pye.
Pike roast.

2.

Lamb in Joints.
Ragou of Sweet-breads.
Stewed Pippins.
Potted Eels.

1.

Soop-Major.
Oatmeal-pudding re-
  move.
Salmon petty, fresh
  Carp.
Neck of Veal.

2.

Ducks or Partridges.
Oat-cakes fried.
Oysters scolloped.
Primrose-leaves friga-
  seed.

1.

Veal ragowed.
Rabbets frigaseed.
A Marrow-pudding.
Salomongundy.

2.

Turkeys with Eggs.
Oysters-loaves.
Potted Woodcocks.
Apple-pye.

1.

Pigeons boiled with
  Bacon.
Limon-pudding.
Sheep's-Tongues friga-
  seed.
Beef boiled.

2.

Chicken roast.
A Tansey.
Roast Sweet-breads.
Potted Eels.

1. For

I.

Forced Tongues.	*Pike roaft.*
Boiled Fowls.	*Calf's-head.*
Beef roaft.	*Apple-pudding.*
Stabe-pye.	*Roaft Tongues.*

2.

Pigeons roaft and larded.	*Lamb roaft.*
	Pan-cakes.
Goosberry-tarts.	*Collar'd-beef.*
Ragou of Lamb-ftones.	*Sturgeon.*
Potted Eels or Trouts.	

NOVEMBER.

1.

Salmon boiled with Whitings.	*Fruit pudding.*
	Beans and Bacon.
Rabbets frigafeed.	2.
Phillet of Veal roaft.	*Lamb roaft.*
Pafty of Venifon.	*Artichokes.*
Beans and Bacon.	*Butter'd Apple-pye.*
2.	*Sliced Tongues.*
Ducks roaft.	*Sturgeon.*
Chine of Salmon boiled with Fennel.	I.
	Chicken & Goosberries.
Peafe.	*Lamb frigafeed.*
Tongues.	*Fawn roaft.*
Black Caps.	*Pudding baked.*
	Loin of Veal roaft.
I.	2.
Boiled Rabbets with Turnips.	*Rabbets roaft.*
	Afparagus.
Veal-cutlets.	*Tarts.*
Hanch of Venifon roaft.	*Pan-cakes.*

Col

Collar'd beef.

1.

Hog's-head boiled with
  Chicken.
Leg of Mutton forced.
Loin of Veal roaſt.
Sweet Lamb-pye.
Frigaſee of Rabbets.

2.

Green-Geeſe.
A Hedge-hog.
Larks roaſt.
Neats-Tongues.
Sturgeon.

1.

Turkeys boiled with
  Marrow-bones.
Frigaſee of Trouts.
Loin of Veal roaſt.
Bacon Frigaſee.
Mutton in Cutlets.

2.

Green Geeſe.
Roaſt Sweet-breads.
Pig's Petty-toes.
Cold Tongues.
Strawberries and
  Cream.

DECEMBER.

1.

Lamb boiled with Spi-
  nage.
Paſty of Veniſon.
Marrow-pudding.
Jiblet-pye.
Roaſt Mutton.

2.

Turkeys roaſt,
Tanſey.
Peaſe.
Cold Tongues.
Strawberries and
  Cream.

1.

Veal ragoued.

Mutton boiled.
Beef roaſt.
Orange-pudding.
Chicken frigaſeed,

2.

Lamb roaſt.
Salamongundy.
Rabbets roaſt,
Goosberry-fool.
Sturgeon.

1.

A Pottage.
Lamb forced remove.
Pike roaſt, Weſtphalia-
  Ham.
Lamb pye and Pigeons.
             Mutton

Mutton roaſt.

2.

Ducks roaſt.
Cheeſe cakes.
Pedſe.
Rabbets roaſt.
Lobſters and Crabs.

2.

Lamb's-neck Alamode.
Leg of Veal and Bacon.
Spinage-pudding.
Griskins of Mutton.
Sallets of Pickles.

2.

Roaſt Lamb.
Kidney-Tarts.

Veal collar'd.
Rabbets roaſt.
Cuſtards in Pots.

1.

Mutton ſtewed,
Lamb's-head boiled.
Veal roaſt.
Rabbets frigaſeed.
Beef boiled.

2.

Chickens roaſt.
Apple-fritters.
Potted Beef.
Roaſt Lamb.
Salamongundy.

1. *How to make a good stiff Cake.*

TAKE a quarter of a Peck of Flour dried in an Oven, put into it a little Cloves, Mace, Nutmeg and Salt; then wet it with one pound of Butter, one pint of Cream; melt it together; beat it very well with a pint of Barm, ten Eggs, leave out half the Whites, a Glass of Sack, a little Rose-water; mix it up very soft; then lay it by the Fire to rise; then work in three pound of Currans, four Ounces of Orange-peel, and Citron candied, three pound of Sugar; bake it in a Hoop, and paper the Hoop, and butter the Paper before it goes into the Oven; Ice it over with three Whites of Eggs; froth it with a Rosemary Sprig; put in half a pound of Sugar beaten in a Mortar; just set it into the Oven again to harden.

2. *How to make Shrewsbury cakes.*

Take two pound of Sugar, two pound of Flour, a few Carraway seeds; take good sweet Butter; beat it with your Hand till it becomes like Cream, a very little Barm; mix it like a Paste, and make it into little thin Cakes; they will bake in a quarter of an Hour.

3. *How*

3. *How to make a good Seed-cake.*

Take a quarter of a Peck of Flour, two pound of Butter beaten to a Cream, a pound and three quarters of fine Sugar, one Ounce of Carraway-feeds, three Ounces of candied Orange-peel and Citron, ten Eggs, leave out half the Whites, a little Rofe-water, a Glafs of Sack, a little Cloves, Mace and Nutmeg, a little new Barm, and half a pint of Cream; mix it up and lay it by the Fire to rife; then bake it in a Hoop, and butter your Paper: When it is baked, ice it over with Whites of Eggs, and Sugar, and fet it in again to harden.

4. *How to make very good Cakes.*

Take half a Peck of fine Flour, five pound of Currans, one pound of Carraway-Comfits, half a pound of Marmalade of Oranges, a dozen Eggs, leave out half the Whites, one pound of Butter, half a pint of Sack, a little Rofe-water, Cloves, Mace and Nutmeg; mould them together with a little new Ale-yeaft, and as much Cream as will make them up into Cakes; then ice them with Sugar and Whites of Eggs, aud bake them in a gentle Oven.

5. *How to make Jumballs.*

Take a pound of fine Flour, and as much white Sugar; mix them into a Pafte with
the

the beaten Whites of Eggs; put to the Paſte
a pound of blanched Almonds well beaten,
and half a pound of ſweet Butter: add half
a pint of Cream, and ſo mould it all well
together, with a little Roſe-water; ſhape
them into Forms, and bake them in a gentle
Oven.

6. *How to make* Macarooms.

Take one pound of white Sugar, one pound
of blanched Almonds, and a little Roſe-
water; beat them in a Mortar; put in a little
Flour, and put it in a Pewter-diſh over a
Chafing-diſh of Coals; ſtir them till they
come clear from the Diſh; put in a Grain of
Musk; then lay them on buttered Papers,
longiſh: Ice them over with Loaf-ſugar.

7. *How to make Bisket-drops.*

Take one pound of Sugar, four Yolks of
Eggs, and two Whites, a little Sack, and beat
it well together one Hour; and when the
Oven is ready put in a few Seeds, and one
pound of Flour, and beat them well together; then butter Paper and drop it on;
then put them in a gentle Oven, and as you
ſet, Ice them with fine Sugar.

8. *How to make Biskets.*

Take one pound of fine Sugar, eight Eggs,
ſome Sack, a little Roſe-water; beat them
one Hour till the Oven is ready; put in one
pound

pound of Flour, and half an Ounce of Coriander-ſeeds; beat it well together; butter your Pan, and put it into the Oven half an Hour; then turn it, and bruſh it over the Top with a little of the Eggs, and Sugar, that you muſt leave out at firſt, and ſet it in again a quarter of an Hour.

9. *How to make very good Ginger-bread.*

Take three Quarts of Flour, two pound of Treacle, half a pound of Sugar, two Ounces of candied Orange-peel, and Limon, one Ounce of Ginger and new Spice together: Mix theſe all together as ſtiff as it can well be made; bake it in an Oven with white Bread.

10. *How to make French-bread.*

Take a Quart of Flour, three Eggs, a little Barm, and a little Butter; mix them with the Flour very light, with a little new Milk warm'd; then lay it by the Fire to riſe; then make it into little Loaves; flour it very well, and bake it in a quick Oven.

11. *To make Quiddany of Plumbs, Apples, Quinces or any other Fruits.*

Take a Quart of the Liquor of preſerved Fruit, and add a Pound of the Fruit raw, ſeparated from the Stone, Rind or Core; boil it up with a pound of Sugar, till it will ſtand upon a Knife-point like a Gelly.

12. *To*

12. *To make a Conserve for Tarts of any Fruit that will keep all the Year.*

Take the Fruit you intend to keep, peel off the Rind, and remove the Stone or Core; then put 'em into a Pot, and bake them with a small quantity of Water and Sugar; being baked, strain them through a strong Cloth; and adding Cinnamon, Sugar and Mace very finely searsed; boil them on a gentle Fire, till they become as thick as a Gelly; and then put them up in Pots and Glasses stopped close, and they will have their proper Taste at any Time.

13. *How to preserve Medlars.*

Take the Fruit and scald it in fair Water, till the Skin may easily be taken off, then stone them at the head, and add to each pound a pound of Sugar, and let them boil till the Liquor become ropy; at that time take them off, and set them by for Use.

14. *To make Sweet-meats of any Apples.*

Make your Jelly of those that are most soft and pleasant; then cutting other Apples round ways, put them into a Glass or Pot, and let them stand six Days; then boil them with the Addition of a quarter of a pound of Sugar to a pound of Liquor, not breaking, but seasoning them farther with the Juice of Limons, Oranges, Cloves, Mace, and perfuming them With a Grain of Musk.

15. *How*

15. *How to preserve Mulberries.*

Srrain two quarts of the Juice of Mulberries, and add to it a pound and half of Sugar; boil them together over a gentle Fire, till they become in a manner a Syrup, then put it into three Quarrs of Mulberries, not over ripe; and after they have had one boil take them out; and put them together with the Liquor into an Earthen veffel; ftop them clofe, and keep them for your Ufe.

16. *How to preserve Goosberries.*

Take them before they be over ripe; cut off their ftalks, and Tops: And if you have leifure, ftone them; then laying in a Earthen veffel a Layer of Sugar, lay upon it a Layer of Goosberries, and fo do between every Lay, till your Veffel is almoft full; then add about a pint of Water to fix pound of Goofberries; and the Goosberries having before been fcalded, fet them in this manner over a gentle Fire, and let the Sugar melt; when being boiled up, you muft ftop them up for your Ufe.

17. *To preserve Cherries.*

Take your Cherries when they are in the prime, and fcattering fome Sugar and Rofewater in the bottom of your Preferving-pan, put them in by Degrees, ftill cafting in your Sugar, remembring you put an equal weight

of

of either; and being fet on a quick Fire, you may add a pint of White-wine if you would have them plump, and when you find the Syrup boiled up fufficiently, take them off, and put them into your Gally-pots for Ufe.

18. *To preferve Green Walnuts.*

Obferve to gather them on a dry Day before they have any hard Shell; boil them in fair Water, 'till they have loft their bitternefs; then put them in cold Water, and peel off their Rind, and lay them in your Preferving-pan, with a Layer of Sugar to the weight of the Nuts, and as much Water as will wet it; fo boil them up over a gentle Fire, and again, being cooled do it a fecond time, and put them by for your Ufe; this Way Nutmegs, when in their Green Husks, are preferved.

19. *How to preferve Apricocks.*

Obferve when they are moderately ripe, to pare and ftone them, laying them a Night in your Preferving-pan amongft Sugar it being laid in Lays; and in the Morning put a fmall quantity of fair Water or White-wine, and fet them on Embers, and by increafing a gentle Fire melt the Sugar; when being a little fcalded take them off, and letting them cool fet them on again, and boil them up foftly till they are tender and well coloured, at that time take them off, and when

they

they are cool put them up in Glasses or Pots for your Use.

20. *To preserve Green Pippins.*

Observe to gather them on a dry Day, before they are too ripe, chusing the Greenest; pare them, and boil 'em in Water 'till they are exceeding soft; then take out the Cores, and mingle the Pulp with the Water, ten Pippins, and two pound of Sugar, being sufficient to boil up a Bottle of Water; and when it's boiled to a thickness, put in the Pippins you intend to preserve, and let them boil 'till they contract a Greener Colour than natural, and in this manner you may preserve Plumbs, Peaches, Quinces, or any thing of that Kind, that you have a Desire to have Green and pleasant.

21. *How to preserve Barberries.*

Observe you gather the fairest Bunches, in a dry Day, and boil several Bunches in a Pottle of Claret 'till they are soft: Strain them, then add six pound of Sugar, and a quart of Water; boil them up to a Syrup, and put your Barberries scalded into the Liquor, and they will keep all the Year round.

22. *How to preserve Pears.*

Observe that you gather them that are sound, not over-ripe, and lay at the Bottom of an Earthen-pan a Laying of Vine-leaves, lay

lay another Laying of Pears upon them, and fo do 'till the Pot is full; then to a pound of Pears, add half a pound of Sugar, and as much fair Water as will diffolve it over a gentle Fire, where fuffering them to boil 'till they are fomewhat foft; then fet them by for Ufe.

23. *To preferve Black Cherries.*

Pluck off the Stalks, of about a Pound, boil them in Sugar and fair Water, 'till they become thick like a Pulp; then put in your other Cherries, with Stalks, remembring you put half a pound of Sugar to every pound of Cherries; when finding the Sugar to be boiled up to that thickness, that it will rope, take them off and fet them by, ufing them as you fee convenient.

24. *To preferve Eringo Root.*

Take of the Roots that are fair, two Pound, wafh and cleanfe them; then boil them over a gentle Fire very tender; after that, peel off the outmoft Rind, but beware of breaking them; after they have lain a while in cold Water, put them into your Sugar boiled up to a Syrup, allowing to each pound of Sugar three quarters of a Pound of Roots; which boiling a fhort time over a gentle Fire, you may fet by to cool, and then put them by for Ufe.

25. *To*

25. *To Conserve or keep any sort of Flowers, as Rofes, Voilets, Cowflips, Gilly-flowers, and fuch.*

Take your Flowers well blown, and clean picked, bruife them very fmall in a Mortar, with three times the weight of Sugar; after which take them out and put them into a Pipkin; and having thoroughly heated 'em over the Fire, put the Conferves up in Gally-pots for Ufe.

26. *To Conferve Strawberries.*

Strain them being firft boiled in fair Water, add boil the Pulp in White-wine and Sugar, as much as is convenient to make 'em ftiff; and thus you may conferve any fort of Fruit; the difference not being great between this, and making Fruit-pafte; of which I fhall fpeak heareafter.

27. *How to Candy Ginger.*

Take the faireft Pieces, pare off the Rind, and lay them in Water twenty-four Hours; and having boiled double-refined Sugar to the height of Sugar again; when it begins to be cold put in your Ginger, and ftir it 'till it is hard to the Pan: Then taking it out piece by piece, laying it by the Fire; and afterwards put it into a warm Pan, and tye it up clofe, and the Candy will be firm.

28. *To*

28. *To candy Cherries.*

Take them before they are full ripe, ſtone them; and having boiled your fine Sugar to a height, pour it on them gently, moving them; and ſo let them ſtand 'till almoſt cold, and then take 'em out and dry 'em by the Fire.

29. *To candy Elicampane-roots.*

Take them from the Syrup in which they have been preſerved, and dry them with a Cloth; and for every pound of Roots, take a pound and three quarters of Sugar, boil it to a height, and dip your Roots into it, when hot, and they will take it well.

30. *To candy Barberies,*

You muſt take them out of the Preſerve, and waſh off the Syrup in warm Water; then ſift fine Sugar on them, rnd put them in an Oven, or over a Stove to dry them, ſtirring or moving them the mean while, and caſting more Sugar upon 'em till they are dry.

31. *To candy Grapes.*

You muſt take them after they are Preſerved, and uſe them as the former.

32. *To candy Eringo-roots.*

Take the Roots pared and boiled to a convenient ſoftneſs, and to each pound add two pound of fine Sugar; clarifie it with Whites of Eggs, that it may be tranſparent; and
being

being boiled to a height dip in your Roots, two or three at once; and afterwards dry 'em in an Oven or Stove, for your ufe: And in this Fafhion you may candy any thing, as Fruit or Roots, to which Candying is proper; and as for Flowers which that way are pleafant and ornamental, you candy them after the following manner, with their Stalks and Leaves. Take your various forts of Flowers, cut the Stalks if they are very long, somewhat fhorter; and having added about eight spoonfuls of Rofe-water to a pound of white Sugar boil it to a Clearnefs; and as it begins to grow ftiff and cool, dip your Flowers into it; and take them out prefently, lay them one by one in a Sieve, and hold it over a Stove, and they will dry and harden.

33. *To dry Plumbs, Pears, Apples, Grapes, or the like.*

You muft firft preferve them; then wafh or wipe them; after which fet them upon Tin-plates in a Stove, or for want of it an Oven, not too hot, and turn them as you fee occafion; obferving ever to let them have their Stalks on.

34. *To make each fort of Comfits, vulgarly called covering Seeds with Sugar.*

You muft provide a Pan of Brafs or Tin to a good Depth, made with Ears to hang over

over a Chaffing-diſh of Coals with a Ladle,
and Slice of the ſame Metal ; then cleanſe
your Seeds from Droſs, and take the fineſt
Sugar well beaten ; put to each quarter of
a pound of Seeds, two pound of Sugar, the
Seeds being firſt dried, and your Sugar melted in this order; put into the Pan three
pound of Sugar, adding a Pint of Spring-
water, ſtirring it 'till it be moiſtned, ſuffer-
ing it to boil, and ſo from your Ladle let it
drop upon the Seeds, and keep the Baſon
wherein they are continually moving, and
between every Coat rub and dry them as
well as may be ; and when they have taken
up the Sugar, and by Motion are rolled into order, dry them in an Oven, or before
the Fire, and they will be hard and white.

35. *To make artificial Oranges and Limons.*

Take Moulds of Alabaſter made in three
pieces ; bind two of them together, and let
them lie in the Water an Hour or two, boiling to an height, in the mean time as much
Sugar as will fill them ; the which being
poured into the Mould, and the Lid put
quickly on it, by ſuddenly turning, it will
be hollow ; and ſo in this Caſe to the Colour
of the Fruit you caſt, you muſt colour your
Sugar in boiling it.

36. *To make Marmalade of Oranges.*

Pare your Oranges as thin as may be, and
I 4   let

let them boil till they are ſoft in two or
three Waters; then take double the number
of good Pippins, divide them and take out
the Core, boil them to a Pap without loſing
their Colour, ſtrain the Pulp, and put a
pound of Sugar to every pint; then take out
the Pulp of the Oranges, and cut the Peel,
and boil it till it is very ſoft; bruiſe it in
the Juice of three Limons, and boil it up to
a thickneſs with your Apple-pap, and half a
pint of Roſe-water.

37. To make *Marmalade of Grapes*.

Take the ripeſt Grapes gathered in a dry
Day; ſpread them upon a Table where the
Air and the Sun may come at them; after
which take from them the Stalks and Seeds
boiling the Husk and Pulp, or Juice in a
Pan, with often skiming, whilſt it is reduc'd
to a third part; and then let the heat be gentle, and when you find it thickned, ſtrain it
through a Sieve, and boiling it once more,
add a ſmall quantity of fine Sugar, or the
Powder of white Sugar-candy, and ſo put
up into Pots covered with Paper for Uſe.

38. To make *Paſte of Cherries*.

Boil the Cherries till they come to be
very ſoft, and ſtrain the Pulp through a fine
Sieve, and add a pound of Sugar to a pint:
ſtiffen it with Apple-pap, and boil it up to
a height; then ſpread it upon Plates and dry
it.   39. To

39. *To make Honey of Mulberries.*

Take the Juice of Black Mulberries, and add to a pound and half of their Juice two pound of clarified Honey, and boil 'em up with often skimming, till one part be confumed.

40. *To make Jelly of Quinces, Currans, or Goosberries.*

Take the Fruit and prefs out the Juice clarifie it, and add to each Quart a pound of Sugar clarified and boiled up to Candy-height; then boil them, add a pint of White-wine, wherein an Ounce of Cherry-tree or Plumb tree Gum has been diffolved, and it will make it perfect Jelly.

41. *To make Limon cakes.*

Take fine Sugar half a Pound to two Ounces of the Juice of Limon, and the like quantity of Rofe-water; boil them up 'till they become like Sugar; then grate into 'em the Rind of hard Limons; and having well incorporated them, put them up for Ufe in Glaffes or Pots being cold, and cover them with Paper.

42. *To make Red Quince cakes.*

Take the Syrup of Quinces and Barberries of each a quart; cut into it about twelve Ounces free from Rind and Cores; boil them
'till

'till they are very ſoft; then ſtrain the Pulp
or Liquor-part, and boil it up with ſix pound
of Sugar, 'till it be Candy-proof; then take
it out and lay it upon Plates, as thin as you
think convenient to cool.

43. Clear or tranſparent Quince-cakes are made thus:

Take a Pint of the Syrup of Quinces, and
a Quart of that of Barberries; boil and clarifie them over a gentle Fire, keeping them
free from ſcum; then add a pound and half
of Sugar to the Juice, candying as much
more, and putting it in hot, and ſo keeping it ſtirring till it be near cold, at that
time ſpread, and cut it into Cakes as the
former.

44. To make *Marmalade* the Italian *Faſhion*.

Take about thirty Quinces, pare them,
take out their Cores, and put to them a
Quart of Water and two Pound of Sugar;
boil them 'till they are ſoft; then ſtrain the
Juice and the Pulp, and boil them up with
four pound of Sugar 'till they are become
ſufficient thick.

45. To make White Quince-cakes.

Clarifie your Sugar with Whites of Eggs,
putting to two pound, a quarter of a pint of
Water; which being boiled up add dry Sugar, and heighten it to a Candy; then the
Quinces

Quinces being pared, cored and fcalded, beat to Pulp, and put them into the boiling Sugar, not fuffering them to boil long before you take them off, and lay them on Plates to dry.

46. *How to make a Leach of Almonds.*

Take half a pound of Almonds blanched, beat them in a Mortar, and add a pint of new Milk, and ftrain them; add two fpoonfuls of Rofe-water, and a Grain of Musk, with half an Ounces of the whiteft Ifingglafs, and ftrain them a fecond time for your Ufe.

47. *To make one fort of Macaroons.*

Blanch a convenient Quantity of Almonds, by putting them into hot Water; beat them fine in a Mortar, ftrewing on them fine Sugar as you beat them; and when they are well mixed, add the Whites of Eggs and Rofe-water; and when they are of a convenient Thicknefs, drop them off Wafers laid on Tin-plates, and bake them in a gentle Oven.

48. *To make an Almond Syllabub.*

Take new Milk a Gallon, the Flour of Sweet Almonds half a pound, a little Rofewater, two Ounces of Lime-juice, half a Pint of the Juice, of Strawberries, and a Quart of Canary-wine, with two pound of Sugar;

Sugar; beat them, and ftir them together till they froth, and become of a pleafing Colour.

49. How to dish up a Dish of Fruit with preserved Flowers.

Take a large Difh, cover it with another of the fame bignefs, and place the uppermoft over with Pafte of Almonds, inlaid with red, white, blue, green Marmalade in the Figure of Flowers and Banks; then take the Branches of candied Flowers, and fix them upright in order, and upon little Bufhes erected, and covered with Pafte: Fix your preferved and candied Cherries, Plumbs, Peafe, Apples, Goosberries, Currans and the like, each in their proper Place; and for Leaves you may ufe coloured Pafte or Wax, Parchment or Horn; and this efpecially in Winter will be very proper.

50. A Perfume to perfume any Sorts of Confections.

Take Musk, the like quantity of Oil of Nutmeg; infufe in them Rofe-water, and with it fprinkle your Banqueting-preparatives, and the Scent will be as pleafing as the Tafte.

56. To make Curd-cakes.

Take a Pint of Curds, four Eggs, leaving two of the Whites out; add Sugar and grated Nutmeg, with a little Flour; mix them together,

together, and drop them like Fritters in a Frying-pan, in which Butter is hot.

52. *To make Orange-Butter.*

Take new Cream, two Gallons, beat it up to a Thickness; then add half a Pint of Orange-flower-water, and as much Red-wine; and so being become the Thickness of Butter, it retains both the Colour and Scent of Orange.

53. *How to make an Excellent Junket.*

Take new Milk warm; then add Runnet, and let it cool; then strow on it Cinnamon and Sugar, over that cast Cream, and strow Sugar upon the Cream with Rose-water.

54. *To make a whipp'd Syllabub.*

Take a Pint of Cream, six spoonfuls of Sack, the Whites of two Eggs, three Ounces of fine Sugar, and with a Birch-twig beat it 'till it froth well; skim it and put it into your Syllabub-glasses.

55. *To make Curran-Cream.*

Bruise old Currans in boiled Cream; strain 'em through a Sieve, add Sugar and Cinnamon, and so serve it up; and so you may do by Rasberries or Strawberries.

56. *To make Goosberry-Cream.*

Let your Goosberries be boiled; or for want of Green ones, your preserved ones will do:

do: And when your Cream is boiled up, put
them in, adding Cinnamon, Mace and Nutmeg; then boil them in the Cream, and
ftrain all thorough a Cloth, and ferve it up
with Sugar and Rofe-water.

57. *To make Sage Cream.*

Take a Quart of Cream, boil it well; then
add a quarter of a pint of Red-fage-juice,
half as much Rofe-water, and as much Sack;
half a pound of Sugar, and it will be an Excellent Difh; and thus you may ufe it with
any fweet Herbs, that are pleafant and
healthful.

58. *To make Syrup of Barberries.*

Take your Barberries picked from the
Stalks, boil them to a Pulp, then ftrain and
rarifie the Juice; then boil it up, being fix
Pound, with fix Pound of fine Sugar into a
Syrup; and if you find that it will not thicken it fufficiently, you may add more Sugar.

59. *Marmalade of Prunes, Raifins, Currans, How to make it of an Amber Colour.*

Take your Fruit and keep them in a proportionable Quantity of Water, till by being over a gentle Fire, they become foft and
pulpy; then ftone the Prunes or Raifins, and
put them into as much Canary as will wet
them: After that prefs out the Pulp, and
boil it up with fome Slices of Quinces; then
ftrain it again, and put to each pound half
a pound

a pound of Sugar, and half a pound of brown Sugar-candy in Powder, and so put in the Pulp well mixed and sprinkle Rose-water into a Gally-pot glazed, dry it a little in an Oven or Stove, and keep it for your Use.

How to make an extraordinary Good Sack-posset.

Take fifteen Eggs, Whites and Yolks; beat them very well, and strain them; then take three quarters of pound of Six-penny Sugar, and a pint of Sack; put all together in a Bason, and set it over a Charcoal-fire, and keep it stirring till it be scalding-hot, set a quart of Milk over the Fire with some pieces of Nutmeg, and let it boil: When your Eggs are scalding-hot, pour in your Milk, hold your Skillet very high, and pour it in, stirring it all the while; then take it off the Charcoal, and cover the Bason with a Dish very close, and set it by the Fire-side for half an Hour.

61. *An Excellent Receipt for making El-*
der Wine.

Take five Gallons of Water, and twenty Pounds of Malaga-Raisins; pick them from the stalks, rub them clean, and shred them small: Boil the Water an Hour, and then pour it upon the Raisins, and let it stand ten Days in a Tub, stirring it now and then; then strain it through a coarse Sieve. To five Gallons of that Liquor, put four Pints of Elder-juice, the Berries being first

put

Pints of Elder-juice, the Berries being first put into a Pot, and set in a Kettle of boiling Water. The Liquor being strained, and the Juice being cold put it together, and turn it into a Vessel, and let it work; then bung it up close, and let it stand 'till 'tis fine, and then Bottle it off.

60. How to make very good Vinegar.

Take Spring-water what quantity you please, put it into a Vessel or Stone-bottle, and to every Gallon put two pounds of Malago-Raisins, lay a Tile over the Bung, and set the Vessel in the Sun 'till it be fit for use. If you put your Water and Raisins into a Stone-bottle, you may set it in the Chimney-corner, near the Fire, for a convenient time, and it will do as well as if set in the Sun.

63. How to make an Excellent Mouth water.

Take Honey-suckle-leaves, Columbine-leaves, Strawberry-leaves, Violet-leaves, Bramble-leaves, Plantain-leaves, unset Hysop and Cinquefoil-leaves, one handful of each; boil the same in three Pints of Spring-water 'till it comes to a Quart: Then put in a piece of Roach allum and Honey as much as you think fit; you must take some of the boiled Water, and dissolve the Allum and Honey in it, and then mix all together: This will cure a Canker, or any such fore Mouth.

ADDI-

ADDITIONS.

A Bisque of Fish.

TAKE what fresh Fish you please and clean it very well; then steep it in White-wine Vinegar, whole Spice, some whole Onions, sweet Herbs tied up, one Limon shred, a handful of Salt; cover the Fish almost with Ingredients; let it steep an Hour, then have ready boiling a thing of fair Water, then put in your Fish with the Ingredients on the Fire, and when it is about half enough, put in the boiling Water to it, and this way will make the Fish much firmer than the old way; then fry some of the other in hot Liquor; then a rich Sauce made with Oysters, Shrimps, Mushrooms, two Anchovies, Capers, a Bundle of sweet Herbs, two whole Onions, one stuck with Cloves, Horse-radish scrap'd, Nutmeg, the Juice of a Limon, the Yolks of two Eggs; mix all these together with two Pound of Butter, and draw it up very thick, then dish your

Fish

Fiſh on Sippets, and run over your Sauces:
Garniſh your fried Fiſh with Parſly, Horſe-
radiſh, and cut Limon, and ſerve it up hot:
Thus you may do all freſh Fiſh.

Oyſters grilled in Shells.

Slit and beard them, ſeaſon them lightly
with Pepper, Salt, and minced Parſly: Butter the Scollop-ſhells very well; then when
your Fiſh or Oyſters are neatly laid in,
put in your Oyſters-Liquor and Grated
Bread to cover them, boil them half an
Hour, and brown them with a broad red-
hot Iron, or Fire-ſhovel; you may garniſh any Diſh of Fiſh with theſe, or ſerve
them ſingly. Shrimps are grilled the ſame
way; and they are very good upon my word.

To make a Quaking Pudding.

Take a Quart of Cream, and twelve
Eggs, but force the Whites of them, beat
them with a Spoonful of Flour and Grated
Bread as thick as for Rice-Cuſtards; ſeaſon
it with Roſe-water, Nutmeg and Sugar;
you muſt butter your Cloth very thick, or
elſe it will run out, the Pot muſt boil before you put it in, a Pudding of a Quart
muſt boil two Hours, but if it be but a
Pint it muſt boil one Hour.

To

To Pickle Mushrooms White.

Gather your Mushrooms when little Buttons, in the Morning; wash them and rub them clean with a piece of Flannel in clean Water, and as you rub them put them in more clean Water; then boil them in fair Water, with a little Salt for half an Hour; and then strain them through a Colander clean from the Water, and let them stand till they are cold; and for your Pickle, take Vinegar, Salt, whole white Pepper, some Blades of Mace, and about two Nutmegs sliced, and boil 'em for half an Hour, and when it is cold, then put your Mushrooms into the Pickle, and keep them close.

To pickle Cucumbers for present eating.

Wash your Cucumbers clean, and dry 'em in a Cloth; then take some Water and Vinegar, Salt, Fennel-tops, and Dill-tops, with a little Mace, make it salt enough, and sharp enough to the Taste; boil it a while; then take it off, and let it stand till it is cold; then put in your Cucumbers, clap a Board upon them to keep them down, and tye them up close; they will be fit to eat in a Week's time.

To make a Beef Tansey.

Take seven Eggs, putting out two Whites; put to them a full Pint of Cream, a little

K 2　　　　Nut-

Nutmeg, and a few sweet Herbs, as Thyme, Sweet-Marjoram, Parsly, Strawberry-leaves, shred them very small, then take boiled Beef minced very small, a full Plate of White-Bread grated; mix them all together, and fry them as you do other Tansies, not too brown.

To make an Orange-pudding.

Take the Peel of a large *China*-Orange, mince it exceeding small, and pound it in a Mortar; then take the Yolks of sixteen Eggs well beat with a little Rose-water, and put to it a little more than half a pound of Sugar, and as much Butter being melted, and season it with a little Nutmeg, and put it in a Dish being covered with Puff-paste and lay Puff-paste over it, and garnish it in what Form you please.

To collar a Breast of Veal.

Take a large fat Breast of Veal, and bone it, season it with a little of all sorts of Spice, a little Salt, a little Limon-peel, minced small; take two or three Sprigs of Thyme, with as much of sweet Marjoram stript and shred very small, and strow it thin all over the Veal; be sure to put both the Sweet-breads in, and rowl it hard, and tye it with coarse Tape; so bake it.

T

To pickle Barberries.

Take your Barberries after they are picked, and take your shattered Barberries and boil them in Water and Salt almost strong enough to bear an Egg, let it boil half an Hour, and when it is cold put in your other Barberries, and stop them close.

To pickle Ashen Keys.

Take them when they are very tender, and parboil them in a little fair Water, then take half a Pint of White-wine, and a quarter of a Pint of Vinegar, the Juice of a Limon, and a little Bay-salt, and when it is boiled and cold put your Ashen-Keys into your Pickle; keep them from the Air.

Sauce for Wild Ducks.

Take a little handful of Sage, one large Onion shred very small, season it with a little Salt, and rowl them up with Butter into Balls, then put them in the Ducks, and roast them; then take half a Pint of Claret, in it dissolve two Anchovies; then take half as much Butter as Wine, then thicken them with the Yolks of two Eggs, then put your Ducks in your Dish, and pour your Sauce through them, and pull out your Balls; so serve them up.

To

To Souſe a Pike.

Boil your Pike with as much Water as will cover it, together with a handful of Bay-leaves, and as much Cloves and Mace as you think fit; boil it till it is ſo tender that you may run a Straw through it, take it up and put into the Broth White-wine and Vinegar, and an Anchovy; when your Pike is cold put in the Souſe; it will Jelly to keep it long.

To make a good Cake.

Take half a Peck of Flour, two Pound of Butter, break your Butter very ſmall into your Flour, take four Nutmegs, half an Ounce of Cinnamon, ſix Eggs, leave out four of the Whites, half a Pound of Sugar, half a Pint of Sack, and a Pint of Ale-yeaſt, mix all theſe together with a little Salt, put all this through a Strainer, with as much boiling-hot Milk as will make your Paſte very light; let it lie after you have made it a quarter of an Hour before the Fire, then take five pound of Currans well dried, work them into your Paſte, then rowl out a piece of Paſte for the Bottom, then pour on your Cake, for the Paſte muſt be ſo faſt that you cannot mould it, ſo that you muſt put it into the Oven as ſoon as it is made; then for Candy, take your Whites of Eggs that you left out of your Cake, and two or three ſpoonfuls of Roſe-water, and a pretty deal

of

of sifted Sugar ; beat it in a Stone-mortar half an Hour, so that you may take a Feather and Ice it over as thick as you can ; set it into the Oven again to harden a little, and so take it out.

To make a Carraway-cake fine.

Take three Pound of Flour well dried, put into it a Nutmeg grated, ten Blades of large Mace, finely beaten, also ten Cloves beaten, and a little Salt, then rib in a pound of Butter, and put in a pint of Ale-yeast, a pint of Cream warmed, four Eggs, but two Whites, beat them with two spoonfuls of Sack, and as much Rose-water, mingle it together, and handle it as little as may be, and set it before the Fire to rise for half an Hour, then break it and mingle it in a pound of smooth Carraway-comfits ; put it in a Hoop, and let it stand three quarters of an Hour in the Oven.

To make Winter-Cheese-cakes with Puff-paste.

For the Crust, to a Pound of Flour take three quarters of a Pound of Butter, wet the Flour stiff with Milk and two Eggs, then rowl in the Butter ; and to make the Curd, put five Eggs to a pint of Cream, and grate a little Bisket into it.

To make a Bran-pudding.

Take a quarter of a Pound of fresh Bran half a pound of Meal as it comes from the
Mill,

Mill, three quarters of a pound of Currans, ſix Eggs, a pound of Beef-ſuet ſhred
very fine, Nutmeg it to your Taſte; and if
you pleaſe put in a quarter of a pound of
Sugar, and as much Milk as will make it
pretty ſtiff; boil it in a Bag or Cloth.

To make a Tanſey without frying.

Take the Juice of young Spinage half a
Pint, or a little more, put thereto a Pint of
thick ſweet Cream, and a little grated Bread,
fifteen Eggs, whereof put in but ſix of the
Whites, ſweeten it to your Taſte, and ſtir
it in a Skillet; butter your Skillet a little,
put it over a gentle Fire, until it be ſome-
what thicker than buttered Eggs; then lay
it upon a Warm Plate, and ſet it upon a
few Coals, and with a Spoon make it of
what thickneſs you pleaſe; then let it ſtand
and harden a while, then turn it upon another Plate, and let it ſtand a while on that
ſide; if you have no Limon, then put a little Verjuice, and Butter and Sugar upon it,
and ſerve it up.

To make Sauce for Turkeys or Capons.

Take half a Pint of White-wine, and a
little Gravy, and Oyſter-liquor, and a little
grated Nutmeg, and put to it three or four
large Onions boiled tender and maſhed ſmall
with a little ſmall Pepper, and two or three
Anchovies, minced ſmall, boil it a quarter
of

of an Hour, with a little grated White-bread, and put to it a piece of Butter, and put it to the Fowls being roasted.

To make Sauce for Wild-Fowl.

Take half a Pint of Claret, a little Oyster-liquor, a little Gravy, and three or four Shalots; let it boil a quarter of an Hour, with a little grated Bread, and put to it two Anchovies minced, and a little Butter, and shake it well together, and put it to your Fowl, being roasted, and serve them up.

To make Sauce for Venison, or a Hare.

Take half a Pint of Claret, and a little Oyster-liquor, and put to it some good Gravy, and a large Onion stuck with Cloves, and some whole Cinnamon and Nutmeg cut in slices; then let it boil till the Onion is boiled tender; then take out the Onion and whole Spice, and put to it three Anchovies, and a piece of Butter, shake it well together, and send it to the Table.

To make Sauce for Green Geese or Young Ducks.

Take almost half a Pint of the Juice of Sorrel, and a little White-wine, a little grated Nutmeg, and a little grated Bread, let it boil a quarter of an Hour, and put to it as much Sugar as will sweeten it; if you please you may put in a few scalded Goosberries

berries or Grapes, and a piece of Butter, ſhake it up thick, and put it to the Geeſe, being roaſted. This Sauce is proper for Chickens.

To make Limon Cream.

Take four fair Limons, pare them very thin, and ſhred them very ſmall, put it into a Silver Cup, ſqueeze in all the Juice of the Limons to the Peel, cover it and let it ſtand two Hours, ſtirring it ſometimes; then put to it three quarters of a pint of fair Water, ſeven ſpoonfuls of Roſe-water, or Orange-flower-water, add a little more than half a Pound of fine Loaf-Sugar, ſeven Whites of Eggs, and three Yolks very well beaten; ſtrain it all in a Canvaſs-ſtrainer, and boil it till it be thick, ſtirring of it while it is boiling. Orange-cream is made after this way, only leaving out half the Peel, and putting in a Yolk or two more.

To make a freſh Cheeſe.

Take new Milk, put ſome Runnet to it, let it ſtand till it comes like a Cheeſe, then break it, and whey it, and force the Curd through a Canvaſs-ſtrainer; then ſeaſon it with Roſe-water and Sugar; you may put in the Yolk of an Egg if you pleaſe; and if you let it alone it will be as well; temper it together, and ſo put it into a little Colander to drain, then put it out and pour ſome Cream upon it; ſo ſend it to Table.

To

To make a Dish of Wild-curds, like Almond-butter.

Take of the best Wild-curds, and force them through a Canvafs-ftrainer, and feafon it with Rofe-water and Sugar, and lay it out in a Difh what form you pleafe, and fo ferve it in; but Few can difcern it from Almond-butter.

To make a very good Sack-Poffet.

Take a Pint of the beft Sack, fourteen Eggs, leave out fix of the Whites, and be fure you take out all the Treads; put in one Nutmeg and fome Cinnamon; mix your Sack and Spice very well, and be fure you put in Sugar enough at the firft; fet it on a Chaffing-difh of Coals, and beat your Eggs very well, put them into your Sack, and keep them ftirring pretty faft that it curdles not till it be boiling-hot; then take three pints of Milk boiling off the Fire, pour it into your Bafon as hot and foftly as you can, and keep it very well ftirring till the Milk be all in, then take out your Spoon, take it off the Coals quickly, and cover it one quarter of an Hour; and fo ferve it covered.

To make a Lamb-pye fit for your Lady-ship's Table.

Cut your Lamb in thin flices, and feafon it with Cloves, Mace, Nutmeg, Sugar and
Salt,

Salt, with a little ſmall Pepper, and lay it in your Coffin; and lay on it and between it, a few Raiſins of the Sun ſtoned, and a few Currans, and a few Skirrets boiled and blanched, and the Marrow of two or three Bones; candied Limon, Dates, and dried Citron, preſerved Barberries, and candied Lettice, and ſliced Limon, large Mace and Butter; and cloſe your Pye; and when it is baked, let your Caudle be White-wine, Verjuice and Sugar, beaten up with the Yolks of three or four Eggs, and ſet it on the Fire, and keep it ſtirring till it begins to be thick; put it in and ſhake it together: ſcrape on Sugar, and ſend it up.

To make a Lamb Pye another Way.

Cut your Lamb in thin Slices, and ſeaſon it with Pepper and Salt, and Nutmeg, and lay it in your Coffin, and lay on it large Mace and Butter, and cloſe your Pye; the ſame Way make a Veal Pye.

Carps ſtewed Royal.

After the Carps are killed, and the Garbidge drawn out of their Bellies and waſh'd, then ſteep them in Claret-wine with whole Spice, and whole Onions, Horſe-radiſh, and Limon ſhred, a little Salt and Vinegar; then ſtew them gently half an Hour, or three quarters; then thicken the Butter with Flour in a Sauce-pan; add ſome of the Fiſh

or

or Carps-liquor, two Anchovies, Oyſters
and Shrimps ; then pour it over your Fiſh ;
let it thicken with the Claret, put in ſome
Sippets : Garniſh with the Milt, Horſe-radiſh and cut Limon, or what elſe you think
proper.

How to order Syder the beſt Way.

Firſt ſcald your Veſſels with Water-ſyder,
made of the Parings of the ſame Fruit ; then
to a Hogſhead, after it is thus ſcalded and
very dry, take a Quart of the beſt old *Malaga*-Sack, and put into it ; ſtop it cloſe,
and rowl your Hogſhead up and down every way to ſeaſon it ; then Tun your Syder,
having a Tap in it before you Tun it ; fill
not your Veſſel by a pretty deal, leaving
room enough for it to work in the Hogſhead,
and ſtop it very cloſe to keep in the Spirits,
which elſe will work out at the Hogſhead ;
and as you hear it work, for you muſt every
Day watch it, when it begins to make much
noiſe in working, draw out every Day a
Glaſs to give it vent, otherwiſe it will burſt
your Hogſhead.   And when it is fine draw
it off into another Hogſhead ; and then a-
gain into Bottles as ſoon as you can.

To make Syder as fine as any Wine in Twenty-four Hours, or thereabouts.

Firſt, let your Syder ſettle in the Rhine
for Twenty-four Hours or more, to take it

off from the grofs Lees; and then barrel it
up; and as foon as it is Tunned, take in
proportion to a Hogfhead of Syder the
Whites of fifteen Eggs, beat them to a Froth
and Oil; and when the Froth is fettled, put
fo much fine Scowring-fand into it as will
make it neither too thick nor too thin, about
the Thicknefs of Cream; mix it well together upon the Bung-hole, and pour it into
your Syder; then with a ftick rouze it about
foundly to mix it well together, ftop it up,
and as foon as it is fine, bottle it.

To recover Syder when it is decayed.

Take to a Hogfhead of Syder, Twenty-
four Pound of the beft Frail *Malaga* Raifins,
and put them into your Syder, and in a few
Days it will be fine, and very palatable;
which you muft watch by drawing every
Day a little at a Peg-hole in your Veffel;
but let your Peg be no higher than the middle of the Head of the Veffel, then draw it
off prefently into Bottles, or elfe in two or
three Days it will not be worth a Farthing.

*Another Way much approved to make any Syder,
though quite fowre, if not quite flat and dead,
to be of the perfect Colour and Tafte with the
Red-ftreak. Thus:*

Take in proportion to a Hogfhead of very
pale fowre Syder fix pound of brown Sugar-
candy; then draw off as much of that Syder

dor as in boiling with the Sugar-candy will make a perfect Syrup; then set this Syrup to cooling; and when it is perfectly cold, pour it into the Syder, and stop it very close; it will presently cause a Fermentation, but not so great as to hurt your Syder; your Vessel must not be quite full, that it may have room to ferment, and in a few Days it will be fit to drink.

How to Preserve Pippins.

Take Pippins, and pare, core, and quarter them, and put them into fair Water, take in also some of their Parings, and the Parings of some other Apples, which you will pare and quarter, also in small quarters; and make them boil till they are tender; then put them into a clean Cloth, and let the Water run from them; and then take as much of that Water or Decoction as will serve to boil up the quarters that you have reserved for your Preserve, and put it into a Copper-pan very clean, and put in as much fine Sugar as you please, but in proportion to the quantity of Quarters of Apples that you intend to preserve, put 'em all together and make your Pan boil upon a good Charcoal-fire till they are very tender; striring them sometimes with a Spoon, but not to break them; then take them out, and lay them upon the Brims of a Dish, or on a clean Cloth a running; after this you may

dish

diſh them up upon a Plate, and then make an end of boiling your Syrup upon a quick Fire, putting in ſome more Sugar, and the Juice of Limons, and let it boil till it be a Jelly; then take it off from the Fire and let it ſtand till it is cold; and then pour it over your Apples, and on the Brims of your Plates as you think fit. But remember to take out the Parings of your Apples before you ſtrain the Decoction from your Apples. This Decoction is very good for the doing of almoſt all other Fruits; but ſome will boil the Parings before the Fruits, and ſtrain out the Water.

To make moſt rare Sauſages without Skins.

Take a Leg of young Pork, cut off all the Lean and mince it very ſmall, but leave none of the Strings or Skins amongſt it; then take two Pound of Beef-ſuet ſhred ſmall, two handfuls of Red-ſage, a little Pepper, Salt and Nutmeg, with a ſmall piece of an Onion: Mince them together with the Fleſh and Suet, and being fine minced, put the Yolks of two or three Eggs, and mixing all together, make it into a Paſte; and when you uſe it rowl out as many pieces as you pleaſe, in the Form of an ordinary Sauſage, and fry them. This Paſte will keep a Fortnight upon occaſion.

To dry Neats-Tongues.

Take Salt beaten very fine, and Salt-petre, of each a like Quantity; rub your Tongues
very

very well with the Salts, and cover them all
over with it, and as it waftes put on more;
when they are hard and ftiff they are enough;
then rowl them in Bran, and dry them before a foft Fire. Before you boil them let
them lie in Pump-water one Night, and boil
them in Pump-water.

Otherways powder them with Bay-falt;
and being well fmoak'd hang them up in a
Garret or Cellar, and let them come no
more to the Fire till they are boil'd.

To roaft a Neat's-Tongue.

Take a Neat's-Tongue being tender boil'd,
blanch'd and cold, cut a Hole in the Butt-
end, and mince the Meat that you take out;
then put fome Sweet-herbs finely minced to
it, with a minced Pippin or two, the Yolks
of Eggs fliced, fome minced Beef-fuet or
minced Bacon, beaten Ginger and Salt, fill
the Tongue, and ftop the End with a Caul
of Veal, lard it and roaft it, then make
Sauce with Butter, Nutmeg and Juice of
Oranges: Garnifh the Difh with flic'd Limon-peel and Barberries.

To roaft a Neat's-Tongue or Udder otherways.

Boil it a little, blanch it, lard it with pretty big Lard all the length of the Tongue,
as alfo the Udder; being firft feafon'd with
Nutmeg, Pepper, Cinnamon and Ginger;
then fpit and roaft them, and bafte 'em with
fweet

sweet Butter; being roasted dress them with grated Bread and Flour, and some of the Spices above-said, some Sugar, and serve it with Juice of Oranges, Sugar, Gravy, and sliced Limon on it.

To make Minc'd-pyes with Neat's-Tongues.

Take a fresh Neat's-Tongue, boil, blanch, and mince it, hot or cold; then mince four Pounds of Beef-suet by it self; mingle them together; and season them with an Ounce of Cloves and Mace beaten, some Salt, half a preserv'd Orange, and a little Limon-peel minc'd, with a quarter of a pound of Sugar, four pounds of Currans, a little Verjuice and Rose-water, and a quarter of a Pint of Sack, stir all together and fill your Pyes; in the Figures as on the Copper-plate, *Numb.* 3 or others as you please.

Sauces for Roast Pigeons, or Doves.

1. Gravy and Juice of Orange.
2. Boiled Parsly minced and put amongst some Butter and Vinegar, beaten up thick.
3. Gravy, Claret, and an Onion stewed together with a little Salt.
4. Vine-leaves roasted with the Pigeons, minced and put in Claret-Wine, and Salt, boiled together, some Butter and Gravy.
5. Sweet Butter and Juice of Orange beat together and made thick.

6. Minced

6. Minced Onions boiled in Claret-wine almoſt dry ; then put to it Nutmeg, Sugar, Gravy of the Fowl, and a little Pepper.

7. Or Gravy of the Pigeons only.

Sauces for all Manner of Roaſt Land-Fowl, as Turkey, Buſtard, Peacock, Pheaſant, Partridge.

1. Sliced Onions being boiled, ſtew 'em in ſome Water, Salt, Pepper, ſome grated Bread, and the Gravy of the Fowl.

2. Take Slices of White-bread, and boil them in fair Water with two whole Onions, ſome Gravy, half a grated Nutmeg, and a little Salt ; ſtrain them together through a Strainer, and boil it up as thick as Water-Gruel ; then add to it the Yolks of two Eggs, diſſolved with the Juice of two Oranges.

3. Take thin Slices of Manchet, Gravy of the Fowl, ſome ſweet Butter, grated Nutmeg, Pepper and Salt, ſtew all together, and being ſtewed, put in a Limon minced with the Peel.

4. Onions ſliced and boiled in fair Water, and a little Salt, a few Bread-crumbs, beaten Pepper, Nutmeg, three Spoonfuls of White-wine, and ſome Limon-peel finely minced and boiled all together ; being almoſt boiled put in the Juice of an Orange, beaten Butter, and the Gravy of the Fowl.

5. Stamp Small-nuts to a Paſte, with Bread, Nutmeg, Pepper, Saffron, Cloves, Juice of
Orange,

Orange, and ftrong Broth, ftrain and boil them together very thick.

6. Quince, Prunes, Currans, and Raifins boil'd, Muskified Bisket, ftamp'd and ftrained with White-wine, Rofe-Vinegar, Nutmeg, Cinnamon, Cloves, Juice of Oranges and Sugar; boil it not too thick.

7. Take a Manchet, pare off the Cruft and flice it, then boil it in fair Water, and being boil'd fomewhat thick put in fome White-wine, Wine-vinegar, Rofe or Elder-vinegar, Sugar and Butter.

8. Almond-pafte, and Crumbs of Manchet, ftamp them together with fome Sugar, Ginger, and Salt, ftrain them with Grape verjuice, and Juice of Oranges; boil it pretty thick.

To make Rofe or Elder-vinegar.

Keep Rofes dried, or dried Elder-flowers, put them into feveral double Glaffes, or Stone-bottles, write upon them and fet 'em in the Sun, by the Fire, or in a warm Oven, when the Vinegar is out, fill them up again.

To make Verjuice.

Take Crabs as foon as the Kernels turn black, and lay them in a heap to fweat, then pick them from Stalks and Rottennefs; and then in a long Trough with ftamping Beetlets, ftamp them to mafh, and make a Bag of coarfe Hair-cloth, as fquare as
the

the Prefs ; fill it with the ftamped Crabs, and being well preffed, put it up in a clean Veffel.

To make Muftard.

Have good Seed, pick it and wafh it in cold Water, drain it and rub it dry in a Cloth very clean ; then beat it in a Mortar, with ftrong Wine-vinegar ; and being fine beaten, ftrain it and keep it clofe covered, or grind it in a Muftard-Quern, or a Bowl with a Cannon-Bullet.

To make Pancakes.

Take three Pints of Cream, a Quart of Flour, eight Eggs, three Nutmegs, a Spoonful of Salt, and two Pounds of clarified Butter ; the Nutmegs being beaten, ftrain them with the Cream, Flour and Salt, fry them into Pan-cakes, and ferve them with fine Sugar.

Other Ways.

Take three pints of Spring-water, a quart of Flour, Mace and Nutmeg beaten, fix Cloves, a Spoonful of Salt, and fix Eggs ; ftrain them and fry them into Pancakes.

Or thus :

Make ftiff Pafte of fine Flour, Rofe-water, Cream, Saffron, Yolks of Eggs, Salt and Nutmeg, and fry them in clarified Butter.

Or

Or *thus*

Take three Pints of Cream, a Quart of Flour, five Eggs, Salt, three Spoonfuls of Ale, a Race of Ginger, Cinnamon as much, strain these Materials, then fry them, and serve them with fine Sugar.

To make a Tansey the best Way.

Take twenty Eggs, and take away five Whites, strain them with a Quart of good thick sweet Cream, and put to it a grated Nutmeg, a Race of Ginger grated, as much Cinnamon beaten fine, and a Penny White-loaf grated also; mix them all together with a little Salt, then stamp some Green Wheat, with some Tansey Herbs, strain it into the Cream, and Eggs, and all together: Then take a clean Frying-pan, and a quarter of a Pound of Butter, melt it, and put in the Tansey, and stir it continually over the Fire with a Slice or Ladle, chop it and break it as it thickens, and being well incorporated, put it out of the Pan into a Dish, and chop it very fine, then make the Frying-pan very clean, and put in some more Butter, melt it and fry it whole, or in Spoonfuls; being finely fried on both sides, dish it up and sprinkle it with Rose-Vinegar, Grape-Ver-
juice,

Juice, Elder-Vinegar, Cowslip-Vinegar, or the Juice of three or four Oranges, and strow on good store of fine Sugar.

Other Ways:

Take a little Tansy, Featherfew, Parsly and Violets, stamp and strain them with eight or ten Egs and Salt, fry them in sweet Butter, and serve them on a Plate or Dish with some Sugar.

A Tansey for Lent.

Take Tansey and all manner of Herbs as before, and beaten Almonds, stamp them with the Spawn of a Pike or Carp, and strain them with the Crumb of a fine Manchet, Sugar and Rose-water, and fry it in sweet Butter.

To collar a Surloin, Flank, Brisket, Rand, or Fore-Rib of Beef.

Take the Flank of Beef, take out the Sinews and most of the Fat, put it into Pickle, with as much Water as will cover it, and put a handful of Salt-petre to it; let it steep three Days and not shift it; then take it out and hang it a draining in the Air, wipe it dry, then have a good handful of Red Sage, some Tops of Rosemary, Savory, Marjoram

Marjoram and Thyme, but twice as much
Sage, mince them very fmall, then take a
quarter of an Ounce of Mace, and half as
many Cloves, with a little Ginger, and
half an Ounce of Pepper, and likewife half
an Ounce of Petre-falt; mingle them together, then take your Beef, fplit it, and
lay it even that it may roll up handfomely
in a Collar; then take your Seafoning of
Herbs and Spices, and ftrew it all over, roll
it up clofe, and bind it faft with Packthread;
put it into an Earthen Pipkin or Pot, and
put a Pint of Claret to it, an Onion and
two or three Cloves of Garlick, clofe it up
with a piece of coarfe Pafte, and bake it
in a Baker's Oven; it will take fix Hours
foaking.

To make Soufe or Pickle to keep Venifon in that is Tainted.

Take ftrong Ale, and as much Vinegar
as will make it fharp, boil it with fome
Bay-falt, and make a ftrong Brine, fcum it,
and let it ftand till it be cold, then put in
your Venifon twelve Hours, prefs it, boil
it, and feafon it, then bake it.

Other Soufe for Tainted Venifon.

Take your Venifon, and boil Water, Beer,
and Wine-vinegar together, and fome Bay-
leaves,

leaves, Thyme, Savory, Rofemary and
Fenil, of each a handful; when it boils
put in your Venifon, parboil it well and
prefs it, and feafon it as aforefaid, bake it
to be eaten cold or hot, and put fome raw
minced Mutton under it.

Other Ways to preferve Tainted Venifon.

Bury it in the Ground in a clean Cloth
all Night, and it will take away the Cor-
ruption, Savour or Stink.

Other Soufe to counterfeit Beef or Mutton to give it a Venifon-colour.

Take fmall Beer and Vinegar, and parboil your Beef in it, let it fteep all Night,
then put fome Turnfole to it, and being
baked, a good Judgment fhall not difcern
it from Red or Fallow Deer.

Other Ways to counterfeit Ram, Weather, or other Mutton, for Venifon.

Bloody it in Sheep's, Lamb's, or Pig's
Blood, or any good and new Blood;
feafon it as before, and bake it either for
hot or cold. In this Fafhion you may bake
Mutton, Lamb, or Kid.

Fifh

Fish, when in Season.

Severn Salmon in season from *All-Holland-*Tide till *June.*

Thames Salmon in season from *April,* and allowed to be caught to *Holy-Rood* the 13th of *September.*

Sturgeon catched in the Eastern-parts in *April, May* and *June,* (excellent Fish roasted fresh) but chiefly eaten pickled, most caught at *Hamborough,* and at a place belonging to the King of *Prussia,* call'd *Pillow*; sometimes catch'd in the River *Severn,* and now and then in the *Thames.*

Turbet in season all the Year, but scarce in the Months of *December, January,* and *February.*

Carp Spawn in *May,* in season all the Year, at some Place or other; *Thames* Carp reckon'd the best.

Whitings and *Cod* in season here chiefly in *November,* but in the Northern-Countries longer.

Lampreys in season from *Christmas* to *June* to be Potted, catch'd in the River *Severn.*

Makarels in season the latter End of *April,* and continue *May* and *June.*

Lobsters and *Crabs* come in in *August,* and hold till *Christmas,* which is call'd the first season; and from *Christmas* to *June,* is call'd the second season.

Oysters.

Oysters in season from the Beginning of *September* to *April.*

Herrings in season in *June,* but the biggest season when in full Row is in *September, October* and *November.*

Trouts in season in *April, May,* and the Beginning of *June; Hampshire* the chief Country for them.

Soles, Thornback, Crawfish and *Eels,* always in season.

Fowls and Rabbets, &c. when in season.

In *January, February* and *March,* Turkey-Poults, Green-Geese, Ducklins, small fat Chickens, some Pigeons, tame sucking Rabbets, Pheasants and Partridge with Eggs, are in season. And in *March* Leverets, Wild-Pigeons, Wild-Rabbets. In *April, May* and *June,* the Chicken, come to be large Fowls, so that Turkey, Geese, Ducks and Fowls are in season all the Year.

In *July* and *August,* Wild Ducks that shed their Feathers, which are called Flappers or Moulters, come very Fat; and at the latter End of the Year most sort of Fowls both Wild and Tame are good and in season, as Swans, Bustards, Wild-Geese, Brand-Geese, Wild-Ducks, Teal, Widgins, Shufflers, Penteals, Easterlings, Heath-cocks, Wood-cocks, Snipes, Plovers, Larks, Quails, Black-birds, Thrushes,

Thrufhes, Felfairs, Pheafants, Partridge,
Bittern, Geefe, Tame-Ducks, Cock-Tur-
keys, and Hen-Turkeys, Capons, Virgin-
Pullets, and Hens with Egg, and Chickens;
likewife Hares and Rabbets.

Note, That the Cock-Turkey is out of
feafon after *Chriftmas*, but the Hen con-
tinues in feafon till *Eafter*, and is with
Egg all the Spring.

How to make Gravy.

Slice lean Beef, and lay it in a Stew-
pan with a bit of Butter, and a flice of Bacon; cover it very clofe; and when it is
done add a Ladle full of Jelly-broth, fo
keep it for Ufe; and when you have occafion add fome Catchup.

To burn Butter for any Sauce.

Set the Butter over the Fire in the
Sauce-pan, and let it boil 'till 'tis fo brown
as you like it; then fhake in Flour, ftirring it all the while; fo ufe it for any
Sauce that is too thin.

To make Welfh Sturgeon.

Take a Leg of Beef, and feafon it with
beaten Mace, White Pepper, Salt, Thyme,
Winter-

Winter-favory, Penny-royal, fweet Marjoram, Parfly fhred fmall, with a little Limon-peel, and an Onion as big as a Wall-
nut; take a good Neat's-foot, bone it, and
cut it crofs Diamond-cut, fo lay it together in the Pan, and juft cover it with Wa-
tèr, and bake it tender; and when you have
made a Dinner of it, pick it all out of the
Liquor clean from the Bones, and when it
is cold, fhred it very fmall with a little
Beef-fuet fhred alfo; then beat it in a Stone-
mortar, fo fqueeze it into a Venifon-pot,
and put thereon the Fat that came off when
it was firft baked, fet it in a cold Oven one
Hour.

To make Pottage.

Take a quarter of a Pound of Butter and
put it in the Stew-pan, and let it ftand over
the Stove till it is brown; then fhred an Onion fmall and put into it; then fhake in fome
Flour whilft 'tis pretty thick; then put in
the ftrong Broth by degrees, and fo let it
boil a quarter of an Hour; then put in two
Slices of Limon a little Mace, beaten Pepper, and a little bunch of Thyme, then take
the Ox-pallates and Sweet-breads, cut them
in thin flices, and put in the Pottage with
fome Forc'd-meat-balls; then let them ftand
over the Stove, and as the Fat rifeth fcum
it off; then take three Heads of white Endive and boil it a little; then fhred it and put
it

it in the Broth with fried Sauſages cut in
pieces, and let it boil a little while; then
take a French-Roll, and cut it in thin Slices,
and toaſt it very brown, and put it in; or
you may put in a roaſted Fowl in the Middle of it, and ſo ſerve it up; Garniſhed the
Diſh with Green Endive ſcalded, and ſliced
Limon.

A White Frigaſee.

Inſtead of frying it with Butter you muſt
ſtew it in the frying with fair Water, Salt,
Spice and Herbs, ſo that it is enough; put
it into White-wine, Shalots, Anchovies,
Gravy, let it ſtew a little more; then put
it in the Yolks of Eggs. beaten with White-
wine,, beaten Mace, and a little ſhred
Thyme, Savory, and pieces of Butter.

A General Sauce.

Mince a little Limon-peel very ſmall, a
little Nutmeg, beaten Mace, and Shalot;
ſtew them in a little White-wine and Gravy,
ſo melt your Butter therein; if it be for
Haſhes of Mutton, or Fiſh, add Anchovies,
a little of the Liquor of ſtewed Oyſters, and
Limon-peel.

Pottage in Summer.

Take a Leg or Shin of Beef, the Scrag-
end of a Neck of Veal, or Mutton, waſh the
Meat,

Meat, then chop it in pieces, boil it in two Gallons of Water six or eight Hours, flowly, covered clofe; and when it is half done, put in half an Ounce of white whole Pepper tied in a Rag, and two Onions; and when the Meat is boiled to Rags, ftrain all through a coarfe Hair-fieve, fqueezed hard, and add a little Cloves, Mace and Nutmeg; beat in a very fmall bundle of fweet Herbs, one fprig of each, of Spinage, Sorrel, Beets, or Endive a good handful of each fhred grofs; let it boil a while, then difh it up with roafted Ducks or Pigeons in the middle of it, and fried Balls, Saufages cut in little bits, fmall flices of Bacon fried, toafted White-bread in fquare flices, you may add Gravy, Cocks-combs, and Palates boiled in Water tender peeled, and cut in long bits; in the Spring add Afparagus cut in bits, with long Green Peafe, put in before the Herbs; in Winter, the Pulp of White-peafe; when you difh it, be fure it boils in a Difh, over the Chaffing-difh, before you ferve it up; the fried Combs and Palates boil in a little of the Broth before you put them in the Difh, with Lamb-ftones and Sweet-Breads; or if you pleafe, with fome of the Combs and Palates.

To roaft Venifon.

Beat the Whites of two Eggs with a little Flour, that is fine, and do it over with a Feather

ther two or three times ; then baste it with
Butter and flour it ; boil Claret with Salt,
and add Gravy ; boil grated White-bread
with Claret, Cinnamon, Sugar and Butter.

To Collar Beef.

Take a whole thin Flank of Beef two
Stone and upwards, bone it, pull off the in-
ward Skin, and slash it crofs and crofs, in
the middle, especially where it is thick ; lay
it in Pump-water six Hours ; then salt it
with as much white hard Salt of Salt-petre,
as an Egg mixt with two Porringers of
white Salt; or if your Petre be ordinary,
then salt it with one Porringer of each, rubbing the Salt very well in, and sprinkling a
Porringer of Wine-Vinegar upon it, so let
it lie three or four Days, rubbing and turning it once a Day ; then rinse it out of
the Brine with a Pint of Claret ; then season it with Nutmeg, Mace, Cloves, *Jamaica*
Pepper, and White Pepper, of each a quarter of an Ounce, beaten all together, with
Thyme, Savory and Limon, after they are
washed and stript, a good handful of each ;
also half a handful of Sage, and the Rind
of one Limon, all shred small together ; so
rubbing all these together very well in
all the Insides; Cuts and Clefts, binding it
up with Tape, lay it in a long Pot with the
Claret, lay the Skins and Bones on the Top
to save it.

For

For a Palſey Water.

Take Lavender-flowers ſtrip'd from the Stalks, fill a Gallon Glaſs with them, pour five Quarts of Rectified Spirit of Wine on them, circulate them ſix Weeks very cloſe with a Bladder, that nothing go out; let them ſtand in a warm place, then diſtil in a Limbeck with his Cooler; then put in the Water, Sage, Roſemary-wood, Betony-flowers of each half a handful, of Lilies of the Valley, and Burrage, Bugloſs and Cow-ſlip flowers one handful of each; ſteep 'em in Spirit of Wine, as they be in ſeaſon, till all may be had; then put to them Balm, Motherwort, Spike-flowers, Bay-leaves, or Leaves and Flowers, of each an Ounce, put them in the diſtilled Wine mentioned a-bove, ſteep 'em ſix Weeks, then diſtil as be-fore; then put into it Citron-peel, Peony-ſeeds, dry and husk'd, of each five Drachms, half an Ounce of Cinnamon, Cardonum-ſeeds, Nutmeg, Cubebs, Yellow-ſanders, of each half an Ounce, Lignum-aloes one Drachm, powder all theſe and put all in, then diſtil Spir. vin. as above, then digeſt it ſix Weeks, then ſtrain it and preſs it, then filter it, then put a ſcruple of Saffron, and half an Ounce of dried Roſes in a Sarſnet-bag in it.

Souſe for Brawn.

Half Beer and half Water, and Wheat-bran and Salt boiled well together, and ſo
ſtrain

ſtrain it; and when it is cold add more Salt, and in a Fortnight new boil it.

Liquor for Sturgeon.

Take Beer-vinegar and boil it very well, with a little Salt, and let it be quite cold; then pour it into the Fiſh and cover it very cloſe.

To keep Anchovies.

Cover them two Inches thick with Bay-ſalt.

To keep Mangoes and Bamboes.

Mingle Muſtard and Vinegar and cover them cloſe.

To ſtew Oyſters.

Take a Quart of Oyſters, rinſe them one by one in their own Liquor, with a little Vinegar and White-wine, then ſtrain the Liquor into them; then put thereto Mace and whole Pepper, Cloves, Nutmeg, and a very little Thyme and Savory, a whole Onion and a little Limon-peel, cover it cloſe and let it ſtew very ſlow almoſt a Quarter of an Hour; then make the Sauce with ſix Spoonfulls of the Liquor, Shalot, Anchovies, melt the Butter therein, ſtrowing in a little Mace, beaten Juice of Limon; wet Sippets in the ſtewed Liquor, lay your Oyſters the beſt ſide upwards; crumble the Yolks of two or three

Eggs,

Eggs, fo pour on the Sauce: Garnifh with Limons, Barberries and Greens.

To fry Oyfters.

Pick out the largeft and dry them in a Cloth, beat the Yolks of two or three Eggs with one or two fpoonfuls of Cream, or Milk, and ftir therein fome grated Bread; then dip the Oyfters therein, and fry them in a great quantity of boiling-hot Suet, as you do Fritters, of a pale, bright, brown Colour; you need not turn them, neither need you turn Smelts, if they have ftore of Suet.

To boil a Couple of Carps.

Scale them and gut them, fave the Blood in Claret, and boil them in good relifh'd Liquor half an Hour, make the Sauce with good ftrong Gravy-liquor, the Blood and Claret, a whole Onion, three or four Anchovies, fhred Shalots, a quartered Nutmeg, a Blade of Mace, a little whole Pepper, ftew all thefe together; then melt the Butter thick therein; be fure the Fifh be well dreined before you put your Sauce therein, add Juice of Limon.

To ftew a Couple of Carps.

Scale them alive, wipe them very well with a Cloth, put them in a Stew-pan with a quart

of Claret, a pint of Syder and a little Vinegar and Salt; then ſtab them with a Pen-
knife in ſeveral places, and let them bleed
very well in the Liquor; then take out the
Carps and gut them, and take from the Guts
the Gall, and then put in the Guts again;
then add a bundle of ſweet Herbs with ſome
large Mace, ſliced Ginger, one Nutmeg
quartered, whole Pepper, three Anchovies,
a little Limon-peel; when it is almoſt done,
two Onions, a whole Shalot, a little Gravy,
cover all cloſe and ſtew them half an Hour;
lay the Carps in the Diſh with the Guts,
and Sippets, and thicken the Liquor with
the Yolks of ſix or ſeven Eggs; you may
add a Couple of Eels to ſtew or boil, Oyſters, Shrimps, Juice of Limon, or ſliced
Limon.

To maronet Trouts or other Fiſh.

Fry the Fiſh in ſtore of clarified Butter,
or Oil, or Suet, till they are criſp; then
take them out of the Pan and let them ſtand
till they be cold, take an equal quantity of
White-wine and Vinegar, ſome Salt, whole
Pepper, Mace, Cloves, Nutmeg, Ginger
ſliced, Roſemary, Thyme, ſweet Marjoram,
Winter-ſavory, a Bay-leaf, or two Onions;
boil all theſe together almoſt a quarter of an
Hour, ſo pour it on the fried Fiſh in a Stew-
pan hot, ſo ſlice a Limon-peel, and add a
Pint of Oil, it will keep a Month covered,
with

with Liquor; ferve it with Oil, Vinegar and Limon.

To Soufe Salmon or Trouts, or drefs them hot.

Let your Liquor be Wine, Water, White-wine Vinegar, a little whole Pepper, Mace, and other Spices, one Onion and a little Limon-peel, Thyme, Savory and Rofemary; let thefe boil together a little while, then put in the Salmon or Trout; a Joll of Salmon muft boil half an Hour, the other according as in bignefs; you muft take it out of the Liquor to be cold, and put your Liquor in a Stone-veffel to cool; add more Vinegar and Salt, then keep your Fifh therein; it may be boiled in the fame manner; to either, make the Sauce a little Liquor, White-wine, Anchovy, beaten Mace, Shalot, ftrew a little, and melt the Butter therein; you may add ftewed Oyfters, Shrimps, or fried Smelts; thefe Fifh to eat hot muft be fcalded: You muft garnifh it with Limon, and fqueeze Juice of Limon thereon, for Pike, or fome other White Fifh; you may leave out the Anchovy, and increafe the quantity of beaten Mace, with a little Shalot.

To do a Leg of Pork Ham-fafhion.

Take a Leg, cut it Ham-fafhion, put it in a Tin Dripping-pan, or long Earthen-pot; let

it

it ftand all Night in the Oven, that is, if ye draw your Bread about 12 a Clock at Night, then by 4 a Clock the next Morning take it out, and before it is cold, take half a handfull of Bay-falt, and as much of that you call falt upon falt, rub it well, and make a little hole in the thick part of the Meat, to let the Salt come to the Bone.

Minc'd pyes of Eggs.

Take ten Eggs boiled hard, and cold, fhred them with one Pound of Beef-fuet, feafon it with a little Salt, half an Ounce of beaten Cinnamon, a little Mace, better than a quarter of a Pound of Sugar, half the Rind of a Limon fhred fmall, fix or eight Dates fhred fmall, three Pippins chopt fmall, a quarter of a pint of Rofe-water, a pound and a quarter of Currans, the Juice of an Orange and a Limon, what Sweetmeats you pleafe, wet or dry.

To make Battalia-pye.

Take Veal Sweet-breads, Lamb-ftones and Sweet-breads, cut the large Sweet-breads in proportion to the bignefs of a Wall-nut, or Chefs-nut; take a Calf's-tongue or Lamb's-tongue parboiled a little, fo peel them and flice 'em; fome fliced Calf's-head or Lamb's-head, Scollops of Veal or Mutton larded with Bacon, two or three flit Larks, a few Oyfters plumpt; feafon thefe with Salt,
Nutmeg

Nutmeg, Mace and Pepper; lay these into your Pyes that all places may fare alike; add Balls, hard Eggs, the Yolks of them, and a large piece of Marrow, large Mace, pickled Barberries, and good store of sweet Butter on the Top; and when it comes out of the Oven, boil some White-wine, Mace, and sweet Butter and put into the Pyes; if for a sweet-pye put Sugar in, and leave out your large Oysters and Balls, and add pieces of Potatoes, preserved Lettice, and Suet, with other Sweet-meats. To make the Crust half a Peck of Flour, almost three Pound of Butter, and boiling Water.

To make Oyster-pye.

Make good Crust, raise the Pye thin, let your Oysters be scalded in their own Liquor, White-wine, Spice, Onion, Thyme and Savory, end when they are cold put them in the Pye, with Butter under, and Marrow, hard Yolks of Eggs, a little Pepper and Salt, beaten Nutmeg, large Mace, Barberries, more Butter on the Top; bake it in a quick Oven, then boil White-wine with a little Mace and Butter, and pour it into the Pye.

To make White-pot.

Take three Pints of new Milk, or Cream, the Yolks of five Eggs, two Whites, beat
your

your Eggs with a little Rose-water, Nut-meg, two or three Spoonfuls of White-sugar, slice half a White-loaf very thin in the Milk, and when 'tis a little steeped break it with your Hands, then put in your beaten Eggs, and break it with your Hands; then put in your beaten Eggs and break it a little more; then put in a bit of sweet Butter on the Top, or Marrow if you please; scatter some Raisins on the Top, you may put Puff-paste round the Dish, bake it half an Hour in a slow Oven.

To make Scotch *Flummery.*

Take a Quart of new Milk, mended with a little Cream, beat the Yolks of six Eggs with a little of the Milk, or a little Rose-water, sweeten it with a little White-sugar and Nutmeg, butter a Dish and pour it therein; set it on a Chaffing-dish of Coals over a broad slow Fire, cover it close; and when it begins to thicken strow in some Currans plump'd in Sack on the Top. You must not stir it whilst it is over the Fire; and when you perceive all over, take it off quick and serve it up.

To make *Tansey.*

Take a Pint of Cream, twenty Yolks of Eggs, ten Whites, beat them well, two
Spoonfulls

Spoonfulls of Rose-water, a little Nutmeg, some fine Sugar, Naples-bisket grated, a Pint or more of the Juice of Herbs, fry it with Butter, or stir it in a Skillet till it begins to thicken, then set it in an Oven to settle it, in a Tin-pan well buttered for the purpose; then butter a Plate and turn it out, then squeeze the Juice of Oranges upon it, and strow fine White-sugar on the Top of it, and quartered Oranges round the Dish; if your Herbs be Spinage in your Tansey, you may add a few Wall-nut-leaves beaten with Sack, it doth very well; in Pippin-time half the Eggs and six or eight Pippins sliced very small; the same with a little more Bisket boiled, will make excellent little Puddings to Batter with Rose-water and Sugar.

To make Patty-pasties.

Take the Kidney-fat of a roasted Loin of Veal and shred it small, with a little of the Kidney or Veal; season it with a little Salt, Cinnamon, Mace, Sugar, a little grated Bread, a little Cream, four or six Eggs, half the Whites, a little Rose-water, so blend it together, and put it into small Pasties of Puff-paste, and so fry them in great store of hot Suet, or bake them, or old Sweet-meats in Puff-paste doth well.

*T*₀

To make Fritters.

Take of the finest Flour well dried before the Fire, mix it with a Quart of new Milk, not too thick, six or eight Eggs, a little Nutmeg and Mace, a little Salt, Sack or Ale; beat them well together, make it pretty thick with Pippins, so fry them dry.

To make ordinary Plumb-cake.

Take half a Peck of Flour dried before the Fire, put thereto Mace, Cinnamon and Nutmeg; beat in almost half a Pound of White-sugar, beat in four Eggs, three Pound of Butter; work all these together very well till you discern no pieces of Butter; then put in half a Pint of Sack and Rose-water together; dissolve two or three Musk-plumbs; wet it with a Quart of Ale-yeast, and a Pint of Milk warm, and so work it very well with your Hands upwards; then put in a Pound of Raisins of the Sun stoned and shred; then put in four Pounds of Currans, mix them very well, and cover it with a Cloth, and set it before the Fire to rise an Hour before you set it in the Oven, so bake it in a Hoop, and let it be two Hours if the Weather be cold; save out one Pound of the Butter to be melted, and poured in, and work it before you lay it a rising.

To

To make Cowſlip or Gilli-flower wine.

Take three Gallons of Water, put to it
ſix Pounds of the beſt Powder-ſugar, boil
the Sugar and Water together half an Hour;
as the ſcum riſeth skim it off; when the
time is expired ſet it to cool as you do
Wort; and when it is cool take a large
Spoonful of the beſt Ale-yeaſt, and therewith beat well three Ounces of Syrup of
Betony, then pour it into the Liquor and
brew it well together : then put in a Peck
of Flowers, only the Flowers cut from the
Bottoms, and infuſe them in the Liquor,
being mix'd with the Yeaſt and Syrup,
let them work together three Days covering them with a Cloth; then ſtrain it and
put it into a Cask, and let it ſettle there
three Weeks, or four, before you bottle it
to drink the old Syrup. Each of the Flowers will ſerve as well as Citron.

To make Cowſlip-wine another Way.

Take nine Gallons of Water, put to it
Twenty-ſix Pounds of fine Powder-ſugar,
when 'tis warm, and the Sugar melted;
put in the Whites of ſix Eggs well beaten;
when it boils skim it clean, then let it boil
one Hour; you muſt pour this boiling-hot
upon a Buſhel of Cowſlips pick'd, then cover it cloſe and let it ſtand Twenty-four
Hours, ſtrain out the Cowſlips, and put
ſix

fix Toafts of brown Bread well toafted, and fpread both fides with the ftrongeft thick Ale-yeaft you can get, then put the Juice of fix Limons and the Peel of two; then cover it clofe and let it ftand two Weeks, or three; then bottle it up, and put a Knob of Sugar in every Bottle; cork it well, and in a Fortnight you may drink it, and it will keep a Year; and if you will keep it longer you muft add to your Sugar three pound more.

To *fcald Goosberries.*

Take a Pint of White-wine and a Pint of Water, one Pound of White-fugar, fo fcald as many Goosberries as the Liquor will cover; the fame Liquor will fcald two or three Parcels, fuch Liquor doth well to quoddle Pippins, cut in halves not pared, and difhed with the Liquor; fo you may fcald any other Fruit.

To *make Hedge-hog Cream.*

Take a Quart of fweet Cream, five Yolks of Eggs well beaten, fet it on the Fire; before it boils take three Spoonfuls of foure Cream, give it a boil 'till it is turn'd, then pour it in a Cloth, and hang it up to dry; then take a Pound of Almonds and blanch them, keep fome of them whole and pound
the

the reft with Rofe-water, or Orange-flower-water to keep them from Oiling, then mix the Curd and Almonds together, and lay it in a Difh in the Shape of a Hedge-hog; cut the Almond in four pieces and ftick them thick in the Back to look like Briftles, and put two blue Currans for Eyes, then take a Pint of new Cream, and fweeten it according to your Tafte, and pour it on each fide of the Curd.

To Pot Rabbets or Hare.

Take Rabbets and bone them, and mince them very well, and fine, feafon them pretty high with Nutmeg, Pepper and Salt; and when fo done, take fome Bacon and cut in thin pieces, and lay the Rabbets, and a Layer of Bacon, and fill the Pot up with Butter; let it ftand four Hours in the Oven; when you draw fill it up with Butter, three Couple of Rabbets will do it.

To Pickle Mufhrooms.

Take thofe Mufhrooms that look not black nor red underneath, nor them that grow near a Wood-fide, nor near any Mineral-ground, and peel off the outward Skin with a Knife, and throw them in a Pail of Water, and cut them thro' the middle; and if there be no Worm-hole in them, then they are good;

then

then put them in a clean Pipkin, and put
in a handful of Salt, more or less, according to the quantity of Mushrooms, without any Water, let them stew a quarter of
an Hour, then take them out of that Liquor; and when they are quite cold put
them in Pickle made of Vinegar and White-
wine, and some large Mace, some beaten
Pepper, a few Cloves, a little Salt, a few
Bay-leaves.

French Pottage.

Take about eight or ten Pound of Beef,
and two or three Knuckles of Veal, and a
few sweet Herbs tied up together, a little
Vinegar, and half a Dozen of Anchovies;
boil them in a Pottle of Water, until 'tis
boiled away to three Pints; then strain them
through a thin Cloth, and when you are
ready to use, take as much as will serve
your Turn, and set it over a few Charcoal;
then take a Duck or Pullet, which you
think most in season, and take off the Skin;
then take a few sweet Herbs and shred them
small; then take two or three Eggs, and a
little Nutmeg and Salt, and beat them all
together, then rowl the Duck in them and
roast it yellow, and lay it in the middle of
the Dish; then take some French-bread,
cut Sippets thin, take a little Spinage and
Parsly and cut it together, but not very
small, and put them a top of the Broth and
serve them up.   *To*

To make Snow.

Take the Whites of eight Eggs, a Saucer full of Sugar, as much of Rofe-water, and put in it a Pottle of Cream that is thick, and beat it all together, and as the Snow rifeth take it off; then take a Loaf of White-bread, cut the Cruft, and ftick a Branch of Rofemary in it, then with a Spoon caft off the Snow on the Top, and all over the Loaf; then gild it; it muft be beaten with a Chocolate-ftick.

To pickle Oyfters.

Take two hundred Oyfters, the newer the better, and be very careful in the opening of them, to preferve their Liquor in a Pan; then cut off the ragged black Verge, faving all the reft, which you muft put in their own Liquor, and Oyfters in a Kettle, and boil them half an Hour, on a gentle Fire, often fcuming them as they boil; then take them off the Fire, take out the Oyfters again, and then take out a Pinr of the Liquor while 'tis hot, and put thereto three quarters of an Ounce of Mace, and half an Ounce of Cloves, then fet the Liquor on the Fire, and let it juft boil; then put the Liquor to the Oyfters, and ftir up the Spice well amongft the Oyfters; then put in about
a Spoon-

a Spoonful of Salt, and about three quarters of a Pint of pure White-wine Vinegar, and a quarter of an Ounce of whole Pepper; then let them stand until they be cold, put the Oysters as many as you can well in the Barrel, knocking the Barrel sometimes, then put in as much Liquor as the Barrel will hold, letting them settle a while; thus you may do a greater or lesser Quantity as you please.

How to stew a Leg of Beef.

Break it well and put to it two or three Quarts of Water, a little whole Pepper, Salt, a bundle of sweet Herbs, and let it stew about eight Hours; then put the Meat and Broth out into a Pan; then the next Day set it on the Fire again, and put into it a Quart of Ale, and set it on the Fire and let it boil about half an Hour; then take it off and put it in a Dish with Toasts upon it.

To make a Goosberry Custard.

When you have cut off the Sticks and Eye of your Goosberries, and wash'd them, then boil them in Water till they will break in a Spoon, then strain them, and beat half a Dozen of Eggs, and stir them together upon a Chaffing-dish of Coals with some Rose-water; then sweeten it well with Sugar, and always serve it cold.

To

3. *To make a rare Pudding to bake or boil.*

Beat a Pound of Almonds as small as possibly; put to them some Rose-water and Cream as oft as you beat them; then take one Pound of Beef-suet finely minced, with five Yolks of Eggs, and but two Whites; make it as thin as Batter for Fritters, mixing it with sweet thick Cream; season it with beaten Mace, Sugar and Salt; then set it into the Oven in a Pewter-dish, and when you draw it forth strew some Sugar on the Top; garnish your Dish with Sugar, and serve it always first up to the Table.

4. *To make Curd-cakes.*

Take a Pint of Curds, four Eggs, take out two of the Whites, put in some Sugar, a little Nutmeg, and a little Flour; stir them well together and drop them in, and fry them with a little Butter.

5. *To make a French Barley-posset.*

Put two Quarts of Milk to half a Pound of French Barley, boil it till it is enough; when the Milk is almost boiled away, put to it three Pints of good Cream, let it boil together a quarter of an Hour; then sweeten it, and put in Mace and Cinnamon, when
you

you firſt put in your Cream; when you have done ſo take a Pint of Sack and White-wine together, of each half a Pint, ſweeten as you love it, pour in all the Cream, but leave your Barley behind in the Skillet; this will make an excellent Poſſet, nothing elſe but a tender Curd to the bottom; let it ſtand on the Coals half quarter of an Hour.

To make Ginger-bread.

Take a Pound and an half of fine Flour, three quarters of a Pound of Honey, or Treacle, which you like beſt, half a Pound of Sugar, and half an Ounce of Ginger, beaten and ſearſed: Clarify your Sugar and Honey on the Fire, ſcum it clean; then put it to your flour, and ſome Ci-tron and Orange-peel ſliced; knead it well, make it into Rolls or Knots, lay them on Tin-plates, and give them an Hour's baking.

To make Elder-berry-wine.

Take twenty Pounds of *Malaga*-Raiſins after they are pick'd and rubb'd, but not waſh'd; then ſhred them with a Chop-ping-knife till they are like a Paſte, and put it into a great Earthen-pan; take five Gallons of Water after it hath been well boiled a full Hour, or more; then put all the Water boiling-hot upon the Raiſins, ſtir

it

it very well about, and let it ſtand cloſe covered for ten Days, ſtirring it twice a Day; then preſs out the Liquor from the Raiſins through a Hair-bag, as you do Sy-der; add to this Liquor three Quarts of the Juice of Elder-berries gathered full ripe, and baked in an Earthen-pot tyed down cloſe, and baked with Brown-bread; then run it through a Sieve without any Preſſure or Bruiſe, only the clear Juice, when it is thoroughly cold mix it together, and run it through a fine Hair-ſieve clear; then Tun it up into a Veſſel, and fill it up almoſt to the Bung-hole, ſtop it cloſe and let it ſtand in a warm Place, but not near the Fire; let it ſtand for ſix or eight Weeks till it be very fine, then bottle it up and keep it in your Bottle-racks, but not ſet it on the Ground, it will be fit to drink in a quarter of a Year, but if kept a Year or two it will be the better; this is more wholſome than any *French*-wine, and more pleaſant.

For the Small-pox, or *Meazels.*

Take Poſſet-drink with Marygold-flow-ers and Hart's-horn often, and once in ſix Hours two Spoonfuls of Treacle-water in the hot Poſſet-drink.

Beautifying

* *
* *

*Beautifying Waters, Oils, Ointments,
and Powders, to adorn and add
Loveliness to the Face and Body.*

1. *To make the Hair very fair.*

WAſh your Hair very clean, and then
take ſome Allom-Water warm, and
with a Sponge moiſten your Hair therewith,
and it will make it fair; or you may make
a Decoction of Beech, Nut-trees, the Hair
will become very fair.

2. *Another.*

Take the laſt Water that is drawn from
Honey, and waſh your Head therewith, and
it will make the Hair of an excellent fair Colour; but becauſe it is of a ſtrong Smell, you
muſt perfume it with ſome ſweet Spirits.

3. *To make the Hair grow thick.*

Make a ſtrong Lye; then take a good
quantity of Hyſſop-roots, and burn them
to Aſhes, and mingle the Aſhes and Lye
toge-

together, and therewith wash your Head, and it will make the Hair grow; also the Ashes of Frogs burnt do increase Hair; as also the Ashes of Goats-dung mingled with Oil.

4. *To make the Hair fair,*

Take the Ashes of a Vine burnt of the Knots of Barley-straw, and Liquorice, and Sow-bread, and distil them together in fair Water, and wash the Head with it; also sprinkle the Hair while it is combing, with the Powder of Cloves, Roses, Nutmeg, Cardamum, and Galingale, with Rose-water; washing it very often the Hair will become fair.

5. *To make the Hair grow.*

Take Hasle-nuts with Husks and all, and burn them to Powder, then take Beech-mast, and the Leaves of Elicampane, and stamp the Herb and the Mast together; then seeth them together with Honey, and anoint the place therewith, and strew the Powder thereon, and this will make the Hair grow.

6. *For the Falling of the Hair.*

Take the Ashes of Pigeons-dung in Lye, and wash the Head therewith; also Wal-
nut-

nut-leaves beaten with Bear's-suet, restoreth
the Hair that is plucked away; also the
Leaves and Middle-rind of an Oak sodden
in Water, and the Head washed therewith,
is very good for this purpose.

7. *To take away Sun-burn.*

Take the Juice of a Limon, and a little
Bay-salt, and wash your Face or Hands
with it, and let them dry of themselves,
and wash them again, and you shall find
all the Sun-burn gone.

8. *To clear the Skin and make it White.*

Take fresh Boar's-grease, and the White
of an Egg, and stamp them together with
a little Powder of Bays, and therewith a-
noint the Skin, and it will clear the Visage,
and make it white.

9. *To smooth the Skin.*

Mix Capon's-grease with a quantity of
Sugar, and let it stand for a few Days close
covered, and it will turn to a clear Oil,
with which anoint your Face.

10. *For* Morphew *or* Scurf *of the Face or Skin.*

Take of Brimstone beaten to Powder two
Ounces, mix it with as much Soap that
stinketh, and tye it in a Linnen-cloth, and
let

let it hang in a Pint of ſtrong Wine-vinegar, or Red-roſe vinegar, for the Space of eight or nine Days, either in Face or Body, dipping a Cloth in the Vinegar, and rubbing it therewith, and let it dry of itſelf, alſo drink the Water of Strawberries diſtilled, it certainly killeth all Morphew or Scurf.

11. *For taking away Spots in the Face after the Small-pox.*

Mix the Juice of Limon with a little bay-ſalt, and touch the Spots therewith often in a Day, for it is excellent good.

12. *An Excellent Pomatum to clear the Skin.*

Waſh Barrow-greaſe or Lard oftentimes in *May*-dew, that hath been clarified in the Sun, till it be exceeding White; then take Marſh mallow-roots ſcraping off the outſides, make thin Slices of them and mix them; ſet them to macerate in Balneo, and ſcum it well till it be clarified, and will come to rope; then ſtrain it, and put now and then a Spoonful of *May*-dew therein, beating it till it be thorough cold in often change of *May*-dew; then throw away that Dew, and put it in a Glaſs, covering it with *May*-dew, and ſo keep it for your Uſe.

13. *To*

13. *To take away Spots and Freckles from the Face and Hands.*

The Sap that iſſueth out of a Birch-tree in great Abundance, being opened in *March* or *April*, and a Receiver ſet under to receive it ; this cleanſeth the Skin excellently, and maketh it very clear being waſhed therewith ; this Sap will diſſolve Pearl, a Secret not known to many.

14. *To take away Freckles and Morphew.*

Waſh your Face in the Wane of the Moon with a Sponge, Morning and Evening, with the diſtilled Water of Elder-leaves, letting it dry in the Skin ; you muſt diſtil your Water in *May*, this I had from a Traveller, who hath cured himſelf thereby.

15. *To procure an excellent Colour and Complexion to the Face.*

Take the Juice of Hyſſop, and drink it in a Morning faſting, half a dozen Spoonfuls in Ale warm, it will procure an excellent Colour ; is good for the Eye-ſight, deſtroyeth Worms, and is good for the Stomach, Liver and Lungs.

19, *To*

16. *To make the Teeth White, and kill Worms.*

Take a little Salt in the Morning fasting, and hold it under your Tongue till it be melted, and then rub your Teeth with it.

17. *To make the Teeth White.*

Take one Drop of the Oil of Vitriol, and wet the Teeth with it, rub them afterwards with a coarse Cloth ; although this Medicine be strong, fear it not.

18. *For a stinking Breath.*

Take two Handfuls of Cummin, and stamp it to Powder, and boil it in Wine, and drink the Syrup thereof Morning and Evening for fifteen Days, and it will help.

19. *To cleanse the Mouth.*

It is good to cleanse the Mouth every Morning, by rubbing the Teeth with a Sage-leaf, Citron-peel, or with Powder made with Cloves and Nutmegs; you must forbear all Meats of ill Digestion, and raw Fruits.

20. *For running in the Ears.*

Take the Juice of Elder, and drop it in the Ear of the Party grieved, and it cleanseth the
Matter

Matter and the Filth thereof; also the Juice of Violets used, is very good for the same purpose.

21. *For Eyes that are Blood-shot.*

Take the Roots of red Fennel, and stamp them, and wring out the Juice; then temper it with clarified Honey, and make an Ointment thereof, and anoint the Eyes therewith, and it will take away the Redness.

22. *A delicate Wash ball.*

Take three Ounces of Oris, half an Ounce of Cyprefs, two Ounces of Calamus Aromaticus, one Ounce of Rose-leaves, two Ounces of Lavendar-flowers, beat all these together in a Mortar, searsing them through a fine Searse; then scrape some Castle-soap, and dissolve it in Rose-water; mix your Powder therewith, and beat them in a Mortar; then make them up in Balls.

23. *To prevent Marks of the Small-pox.*

Boil Cream to an Oil, and with that anoint the Whales with a Feather, as soon as they begin to dry, and keep the Scabs always moist therewith; let your Face be anointed every half Hour.

24. To take away any Chill-blains in the Hands or Feet.

Boil half a Peck of Oats in a Quart of Water till it grows dry, then anoint your Hands with Pomatum; and after they are well chafed hold them within the Oats as hot as you can well endure them, covering the Bowl wherein you do your Hands with a double Cloth, to keep in the Steam of the Oats; do this three or four times, and it will do; you may boil the same Oats with fresh Water three or four times.

25. To make the Nails grow.

Take Wheat-flour and mingle it with Honey, and lay it to the Nails, and it will help them.

26. For Nails that fall off.

Take Powder of Agrimony, and lay it on the Place where the Nail was; and it will take away the Aking, and make the Nails grow.

27. For Cloven Nails.

Mingle Turpentine and Wax together, and lay it on the Nails, and as it groweth cut it away, and it will heal them.

28. *For*

28. *For Nails that are rent from the Flesh.*

Take some Violets and stamp them, and fry them with Virgins-wax, and Frankincense, and make a Plaister, and lay it to the Nail, and it will be whole.

29. *Another.*

Anoint your Fingers with the Powder of Brimstone, Arsnick, and Vinegar, and in a short time you will find great Ease.

30. *For the Yellow-Jaundice.*

Take the Juice of Wormwood, or Sorrel, or else make them in a Syrup, and use to drink it in a Morning.

31. *To take away Warts from the Hands, or Face.*

Take Purslain and rub it hard on the Warts, and it maketh them fall away; also the Juice of the Roots of Rushes applied healeth them.

32. *To make the Hair Black.*

Take the Juice of Red Poppy, the Juice of green Nuts, Oil Myrtle, Oil of Costmary, of each one Pint, boil it a while, and anoint the Hair therewith.

33. *To*

33. *To cure a red Face.*

Take four Ounces of Peach-kernels, Gourd-feed two Ounces; bruife them, and make an Oil to anoint the Face Morning and Evening

34. *To cleanfe the Body and make it comely.*

Take of Sage, Lavendar-flowers, Rofe-flowers of each two Handfuls, a little Salt, boil them in Water or Lye, and make a Bath not too hot; in which bathe the Body in a Morning, or two Hours before Meat.

35. *A fweet-fcented Bath for Ladies.*

Take of Rofes, Citron-peel, fweet Flowers, Orange-flowers, Jeffamy, Bays, Rofemary, Lavendar, Mint, Penny-royal, of each a fufficient Quantity, boil them together gently, and make a Bath; to which add Oil of Spike fix Drops, Musk five Grains, Amber-greefe three Grains, fweet Afa one Ounce; let her go into the Bath for three Hours.

Good

Good ADVICE

TO ALL

Englifh People,

By a late

Eminent Phyfician,

To make a Drink themfelves, which they may drink as they drink Coffee, Chocolate *and* Tea, *Viz.*

TAKE a Quart of Spring or Conduit-Water, and boil it till it waftes one third Part, when you have fo done, your Water being boiling-hot, put in twenty or thirty Leaves of good Sage, and half the Quantity of Rofemary, with fifteen or twenty Grains of good *Englifh* Saffron, and let it infufe hot as before, for about a quarter of an Hour clofe ftopped; then pour it out clear from the Ingredients, drink it as hot

as

as you can, taking about a quarter or half a Pint of it at a time, sweetned with a little White-sugar, and question not but the Benefits you will receive from this will be far more and better this Spring and hereafter, than you ever have done by those Liquors that so many commend, or those Spirits and Pills, whose Virtues and Ingredients are only known to him that makes them, who often forceth them upon you by fallacious Arguments for their own Profit; but the Virtues of these Plants are so Universally known to be of such admirable Qualities, that I shall say the less in the Praise of them; but something I shall say of them, That they are the best Plants that grow in this Island, which is a Climate and Country which I may boldly say is so well furnished with Herbs, and Plants, which for Virtue and Goodness is not inferior to any Country in the whole World, and these I have pitched upon are of its choicest Product. Therefore I shall hint at their Virtues only in general, *Viz.* They resist Poyson and Infection, Pestilential Air and Noysome Stinks, strengthen the Brain, Heart and Nerves, comfort all the Vital Spirits, and breed good Blood, expell all Humours which offend the Stomach and Body; in short, it is a general Friend to Nature, and a general Preservative against almost all manner of Distempers,

pers, and efpecially thofe reigning ones of the Scurvy and Agues, which have fo much afflicted People of late. It is no way offenfive, but helpeth and no way hindreth Bufinefs: I put myfelf to this Trouble, to give my Advice for the Good of my Country. Here is no Fee to be paid, and the Charge is fmall.

More

MORE
RECEIPTS
ADDED.

1. *To fry Beef another Way.*

Take Beef fresh or neat, cut it in pretty thin slices; beat it with the back of a Shredding-knife, put it in a Frying-pan only the Lean by itself, with as much Butter as will just wet the Pan and no more: hold it over a very gentle Fire, keeping it still turned, and as the Gravy runs from it pour it out, fry it not too much, take the Fat and fry it by itself, and lay it a top of the Beef; take the Gravy and put a little Claret-wine, Anchovy, Onion, Nutmeg, Pepper, Stew it a little.

2. *To make Goosberry-wine.*

Take two Gallons of Goosberries and beat them in a Mortar, then strain them thro' a

O   thin

thin Canvas, and let it stand in a broad
Pan three Days, then strain it again thro' a
Flannel-bag, and have a pound of fine Sugar boiled in a Quart of Water ready to put
in when 'tis strain'd, and a Quart of sweet
Rhenish-wine, and then strain it all together
over and over, till it be very clear, and so
Bottle it up; and to every Bottle, put in
two or three Lumps of fine Sugar, stop it
close, it will be fit to drink in three or
four Days: The Goosberries must be very
ripe, and the clearest you can get.

3. To make White Marmalade of Quinces, very nice.

Make your Liquor boil before you put in
your Quinces to scald them, let them be
scalded till they be very tender, keeping
them still turning all the while in the Water, otherwise one side will be Yellow,
and the other White, then take them out
and pare them very quick, or they will turn
Yellow, then cut them in thin Slices,
and weigh them, then to a pound of Quince,
take one Pound of Double refined Sugar;
mingle this Sugar with eight Spoonfuls of
Water, stirring it to melt the Sugar, then
put in your Quinces and set it over the
Fire, and stirring it all together, boil it
indifferent fast, Skimming it very well
(which makes all Sweet-meats both fine,
and to keep well) near half an Hour.

N. B.

N. B. To know when all Sweetmeats is boiled enough, after it is fufficiently skimmed, you will find a clear fhining Skim hang upon your Spoon, and then it is enough ; hold your Glaffes a little over the Stuff to heat them, and then put them in boiling hot. Never cover your Glaffes, for it will make your Sweet-meats Candy and Peckt. Tye the Kernels in a Tiffany-bag, to boil with your Marmalade, to make it Jelly the better.

4. *To make Limon-Cream.*

Take four fair Limons, pare them very thin, and fhred the paring very fmall, put it into a Silver Cup, fqueeze in all the juice of the Limons to the Peeling, cover it and let it ftand two Hours, ftirring it fometimes; then put to it, three quarters of a Pint of fair Water, feven Spoonfuls of Rofe-water, or Orange-flour-water, and a little more than half a pound of fine Loaf-Sugar, feven Whites of Eggs, and three Yolks very well beaten ; ftrain it all thro' a Canvafs-ftrainer, and boil it till it be thick, ftirring of it while it is boiling.

Orange Cream is made after this way, only leaving out half the Peel, and putting in a Yolk or two more.

5. *To*

5. *To make Marmalade of Pippins.*

Take of the best right Kentish Pippins, pared and cut into thin slices a pound, Loaf Sugar beaten a pound, strew some of the Sugar at the bottom of your Preserving-pan, and then lay some Apple, and then more Sugar, and so more Apple till all be laid in, laying some Limon-peel between, and after it is boiled tender, then take a pint of Water and pour it on your Apple and Sugar, and set them over a quick Fire; shaking them round to keep them from burning, and keep them down with a Spoon, but do not mash them before they be quite boiled; squeeze in the juice of a Limon or two, and put them in thin Glasses, boil it apace, put in more of Limon-peel than Orange.

6. *To make Syrup of Gilly-flowers.*

Take 600 of Gilly-flowers, cut them off to the White, then take a Quart of White-wine, put it into a Skillet; and when it boils pour it into a Gally-pot, and put your Flowers into it hot, then let it stand upon Coals to keep hot for three Days; then strain it out, and to a Pint of Liquor, put a pound and a quarter of Sugar, you will have almost two Pints of Liquor; boil it to a Syrup, and put it up (when cold) into a
Glass

Glaſs Bottle. You may do it in Borage-Water, inſtead of White-wine, if you pleaſe.

7. *To make red Marmalade of Quinces. The beſt Way.*

Take three Quinces, boil them well in Water, then take a Pint of that Liquor, and half a Pint of fair Water: then take a pound of Quinces, ſcald them, and ſlice them in thin ſlices; then take a pound of Sugar, put half of it to your Liquor, when it hath boil'd skim it, then when you put in your ſliced Quinces, cover your Pan, and let it boil till the Liquor be red, then take the reſt of your Sugar and put it to your Quinces, and let them boil uncovered until they be enough.

8. *To make a Diſh of Wild-curds like Almond-Butter.*

Take of the beſt Wild-curds, and force them thro' a Canvaſs-ſtrainer, then ſeaſon it with Roſe-water and Sugar, and lay it out in a Diſh in what form you pleaſe, and ſo ſerve it in; but few can diſcern it from Almond Butter.

9. *To make a freſh Cheeſe.*

Take new Milk, put ſome Runnet to it, let it ſtand till it come like a Cheeſe, then

O 3　　　　　break

break it and whey it, and force the Curd
thro' a Canvaſs-ſtrainer, then ſeaſon it with
Roſe-water and Sugar, (you may put in the
Yolk of an Egg if you will) and if you
leave it out it will be as well, temper it together, and ſo put it into a little Cullender
to drain, then put it out and pour ſome
Cream upon it.

10. *To make a Carraway Cake.*

Take three pound of Flour well dried, put
in it a Nutmeg grated, two blades of large
Mace finely beaten, alſo ten Cloves ſo beaten, and a little Salt, then rub in a pound
of Butter, and put in a pint of Ale-yeaſt,
a Pint of Cream warmed, four Eggs, two
Whites, beat with two Spoonfuls of Sack,
and as much Roſe-water, mingle it together, and handle it as little as may be, and
ſet it before the Fire, to riſe for half an
Hour, then break it and mingle in it a
pound of ſmooth Carraway-comfits ; put
it in a Hoop, and let it ſtand 3 quarters of
an Hour in the Oven.

11. *To Collar Eels.*

Take your Eels and skin them, and then
ſlit them down the Belly, and take out the
Back-bone, then take Cloves and Mace, and
Pepper and Salt mixt all together, and
ſeaſon them pretty high, not ſo much Cloves
and

and Mace, as Pepper and Salt, but fo much as to give them a good relifh; then Rowl one or two together very hard, and fow them up in a Cloth, and then boil them; and when they be thorough cold, take them out of the Cloath and put them into pickle.

12. *To make Cheefe-cakes. Another way.*

Take a Pottle of new Milk, turn it into a tender Curd, take the Whey clean from it, then work in it half a pound of new Butter, put to it the Yolks of eight Eggs, fix Spoonfuls of Rofe-water, two Nutmegs beaten and ferced, half a Pound of Sugar beaten and ferced, mix all thefe together and put in a pound of Currans, ftir it very well together with a little Salt, fo bake them; let your Cruft be very thin.

13. *To make little Cakes.*

Take a Pound of Flour well dried, and a pound of Loaf-Sugar fine fifted, a pound of Currans when they are wafh'd, pickt and dryed, a pound of frefh Butter well wafhed in Rofe-water; mix the Flour and the Sugar together, then divide it into two parts; fhake in one part into the Butter, and work it with your Hands together, then take the Yolks of fix Eggs, and but the Whites of two, beat them with a good Spoonful of Sack,

then

then put in the Eggs and mingle them well
together, then ſhake in the reſt of your
Flour and Sugar together, then make the
Currans very hot and ſhake them in, beat
it lightly with your hand, Bake them in
Bisket-pans, and ſcrape Sugar when you ſet
them in the Oven.

14. *To make a Cake, another Way.*

Take four pound of Flour and dry it
well in an Oven, and keep it hot by the
Fire, four pound of Currans when they are
waſhed and pick'd, ſet them by the Fire and
make them hot, then take a Pint of thick
Cream, and melt in it a pound of Butter,
then take eight Eggs and beat them well, and
mingle them with a pint of good Ale-yeaſt;
when your Cream is pretty cold, make a
Hole in the Middle of your Flour and put
that in, having firſt put into your Flour a
quarter of a pound of Sugar beaten, and what
Spice you pleaſe, you muſt ſtir your Cream,
Eggs and Yeaſt together with your hand,
then cover it with ſome of your Flour, lay a
hot cloth upon it and ſet it to the Fire to
riſe, and when it works up above the Flour,
then mingle it together with your Hand,
and let another ſtrew in the Currans, and
half a pound of Raiſins of the Sun ſhred
ſmall; make it up as faſt as you can have
your Oven ready, and an Hour will bake it.

To

15. *To preserve Damsons or any other black Plumbs.*

Wipe them and cut them on the Creſed ſide, take the weight of them in Loaf Sugar, put as much Water as will wet the Sugar: ſet it on the Fire till it be melted, then ſcum it; and when it is a little cold, put in your Plumbs, and let them ſtand on a ſoft Fire, near two Hours, keep them hot, but let them not boil: keep out a little Sugar to ſtrew on them, now and then as they ſtand on the Fire; when you take them off the Fire, to ſet by till next day, it is beſt to cover them when they are warm; when you boil them again let it be a reaſonable pace, till you think they are preſerved thorough: then take out the Plumbs into Pots or Glaſſes, and boil the Syrup a little more till it Jellies, and put it to the Plumbs pretty hot.

16. *To dry Pear-Plumbs.*

Scald the Plumbs pretty tender, let the Water be hot when you put them in, then lay them on a Plate to drein; to a pound of Plumbs, take three quarters of a pound of the beſt Loaf Sugar, and three quarters of a Pint of Water, put them together, and let it ſtand on the Fire, ſtirring it till it be ſcalding hot, but not boil; then the

Plumbs

Plumbs being warm, put them into the Syrup, and then let them ſtand a while on the Fire ; then take them off, and twice a Day heat them ſcalding-hot; turning them, and pouring Syrup on them for nine Days; then lay them on Plates or Glaſſes, and dry them in a Stove or in the Sun.

17. *To make Jelly of Pippins.*

Pare and cut half a Peck of Pippins into a Preſerving-pan, put as much Water to them as will cover them, boil it till the Liquor taſte ſtrong of the Apples ; then ſtrain it, and take to a Pint and quarter of this Liquor, a Pound of the beſt Loaf Sugar, boil it quick till it Jellies ; cut Limon, Orange or Citron in thin long pieces, and put alſo the Juice of Limon or Orange, or perfume it like the preſerved Pippin, if you like it.

18. *To make Sugar-cakes.*

Take a Pound of fine Sugar, and five Pints of Flour ; a Pound and a half of Butter worked in Roſe-water, four Spoonfulls of Cream, four Yolks of Eggs; mingle them all together, worked till it be Paſte ; make it into thin Cakes, and bake them upon Plates.

To

19. *To make Bisket.*

Take a Pound of Flour, and a Pound of Sugar and mingle them together, four Yolks and three Whites of Eggs; beat them with four Spoonfuls of Rofe-water, then ftir all till it be well mingled; then butter the Plates, put on the Bisket, ftrew Sugar on them, and when you put them into the Oven, let it not be too hot.

20. *To preserve Pippins White.*

Take Pippins, pare and core them as you do a Quince; and to a Pound of Pippins, take a Pound of double-refined Sugar, and a Pint of running-Water; put in the Pippins and Sugar and Water together, and let them boil very faft, till they look very clear, and the Syrup Jelly; when they are almoft enough put in the Juice of a fair Limon, and a little Musk or Amber-greafe ground with a little Sugar, and tied up in a little Bag.

21. *To make Marmalade of Apricocks.*

Take Apricocks, the ripeft are beft, pare them and quarter them, and take out the Strings, then to a Pound of Apricocks, take three quarters of a Pound of common Loaf-Sugar, fet them on the Fire in a pretty broad Pan, without either Water or Sugar;

ftir

ftir them continually for fear of burning;
let them melt and boil a good pace a while,
then ftrew in the Sugar as faft as you can,
and let them boil very faft, till they look
clear and the Syrup be thick; then put them
into Glaffes or Pots, as you like beft, it will
Candy a little on the Tops; but is efteemed
never the worfe, and is I think the beft way
of doing Apricocks.

22. *To preferve Cherries.*

Take the faireft Cherries when they are
full ripe, weigh them with their Stones and
Stalks; and take to a pound of Cherries, a
pound of common Loaf Sugar, lay fome of
it in the bottom of the Pan: then ftone the
Cherries upon it, and ftrew on now and
then a little Sugar as you ftone them, when
you fet them on the Fire; to two pound of
Cherries, you may put in a quarter of a
Pint of Juice of red Currans, and moft of
the Sugar, only leave out fome to ftrew in
as they boil, which muft be as faft as they
can, fhaking them round fometimes, but
not ftirring them; take off the Scum, and
when they look deep, and the Syrup grow
thick, take them off the Fire, and pour them
into a Bafon, and fhake them a good while
to gather the Scum together, which take off,
the cleaner you get it off, the better they
will keep, and when they are cold, put
them into Pots.

23. *To*

23. *To make* Mead.

Take a Gallon of Honey, and fix Gallons of Water, boil it till the third Part be confumed, be fure to fcum very clean ; when 'tis almoft enough tye a little Nutmeg, and a Clove or two in a Bag, and let it boil in it, and when 'tis cold put it in a Veffel ; and at two Months old draw it into Bottles, and 'twill be ready to drink in a fhort time, being very pretty Liquor.

24. *To make Mead, the beft Way.*

Take fix Gallons of Water, fet it over the Fire, and as it boils skim it clean ; then put into it a fmall handfull of fweet Marjoram, Sweet-brier and Mufcovil, the like of Violets if at the time, put in four blades of large Mace, 12 or more Cloves, and a Nutmeg fliced : let it boil in all half an Hour, then fet it a cooling, when 'tis almoft cold put two or three hot Toafts fpread with Ale-yeaft into the Liquor, and likewife three or four Spoonfuls of Syrup of Citron, or Limon mix'd with 2 or 3 Spoonfuls of Barm, cover it over warm for 24 Hours, that it may work according to difcretion ; then ftrain it thro' a Rainge, and Tun it into a Veffel of a fit fize, and when it hath done working ftop it up very clofe, after feven Weeks if it be clear draw it into Bottles, putting into each

Bottle

into each Bottle a good Knob of Loaf-fugar,
after a Fortnight you may drink it; but
Age makes it better.

25. *To Collar Beef the nicest Way.*

Take three Gallons of Water, three Handfuls of Bay-falt, fix Handfuls of White-falt,
half an Ounce of Salt-petre, and make a
Brine ftrong enough to bear an Egg, the
breadth of a Three-pence, then take a
Breaft of young Beef and bone it, and lay
it in the Brine nine Days, then take it out
and beat it very much with a Rowling-pin,
then feafon it with one Ounce of Mace,
feven Nutmegs, which muft be fhred very
fmall, not pounded, two Ounces of Bay-
berries, one Ounce of fweet Marjoram dry'd
and powder'd, twenty Cloves, one Ounce
of Pepper, two Handfuls of White-falt,
bruifed in a Mortar, mix it all together,
and ftrew it all over the Beef, which muft
be very well dried; then Roll all up very
hard, and bind it hard with a Cloth, and
put it into a Pot to be baked, then take
two Quart of Claret, half a Pint of Vinegar, and a Pint of Water, and put into it,
cover it over with Dough, and put it
with a Batch of Bread in the Oven, and
let it ftand all Night, in the Morning
take it out of the Liquor, and bind it
fafter, and hang it on a Nail till it be
cold.

26. *To make Bisket another Way.*

Take the Rind of one Limon, put it into boiling Water till it be tender, take a quarter of a Pound of Sweet-Almonds, blanch them in cold Water, and one Ounce of Gumdragon, and foak it in fair Water; then take the Limon and pound it in a ftone Mortar, and pound the Almonds by themfelves, putting in as you Pound the White of an Egg, beaten hollow, then put in the Limon and the Gum into the Almonds, and mix it very well together, then take half a Pound of fine Sugar and beat it in the Mortar, with the Limon, Gum and Almonds, afterwards take a Pound more of fine Sugar, and ftir it into it with a Spoon, then roll it up in little Rolls feverally, and lay them on white Papers, and put them into the Oven.

27. *To make a Cake, another Way.*

Take nine Pound of Flour, and a Pound and half of Sugar; one Ounce of Mace, eight pound of Currans after they are wafhed and dried; then take twenty-eight Eggs, with half the Whites, beat 'em with half a Pint of Rofe-water, then take one Pound of Almonds blancht and beaten, with a little Rofe-water, and mingle it with your Eggs, with three Pints of good Ale-yeaft, and put all in the middle of your Flour; then take three Pints of Cream, and two Pound and a quarter of Butter,

Butter, melt your Butter in your Cream, and
put it in warm after your Eggs and Yeaſt:
ſtir it till it be well mingled, then put it in
a Cloth, and lay it before the Fire half an
Hour, then put it in a tin Hoop, with Paper
at the bottom buttered, and let it ſtand in
the Oven an Hour and half, then Ice it
with Loaf Sugar boiled to a Candy height,
or any other Icing as you pleaſe.

---

1. *For the Stone.*

WHen your Pain makes you apt to vo-
mit, drink a good draught of warm
Beer, or of Poſſet-Ale, wherein boil a few
Mallows; and after you have vomited, and
your Stomach beginneth to ſettle, take a black
Flint of the inner part, heat it in the Fire till
it be red hot, and quench it in White-wine,
and drink thereof. This will force the Urine.

And for the local Pain, take the ſharpeſt
taſted Onions, roaſt them in Embers, peel
off the Skins, and maſh the reſt all to pieces,
and ſpread it on a Cloth your little Finger's
thickneſs, or more, and as broad as both
your Hands, and lay it hot to the Place
grieved: this will diſcuſs the Wind, and en-
large the Paſſage for the Stone. And as the
Pain deſcends, follow it with the Pultiſs; you
may have two in a readineſs, and ſucceſſive-
ly apply them one after another, every ſe-
cond Hour, or as you ſhall ſee Cauſe.

2. *For*

2. *Another Receipt for the Stone.*

Take a Pint of Milk, half a pint of White-wine, half a pint of Syder, half a pint of Ale, make a Poffet of it, then take the quantity of a Walnut of Venis Soap, flice it very thin, and put it into as much Spring-water as will diffolve it, being fet over the Fire and kept ftirring, then put it into the Poffet-drink, and take the Yolks of two new laid Eggs, and beat them very well, then put them into the Poffet-drink, and take the Juice of a large Limon, and fweeten it with Sugar, and put it into the Poffet-drink; and when you are to drink it, put in two Ounces of Syrup of Marfh-mallows, and a large Nutmeg fliced, and drink a pint and a half of it when the Pain cometh; lye down on your Back on the Bed for half an Hour, then drink the reft, walking up and down the Room.

3. *A Water for Sore Eyes.*

Take a Pint of the beft White-wine you can get, put into it one pennyworth of *Lapis Calaminaris* beaten very fine, put it into a Bottle clofe Stopped, fet in the hotteft Sun for two Hours; fhake it two or three times, and when you ufe it, dip in a Feather, and with it ftrike the Lafh of your Eye once

or

or twice, firſt ſhaking the Glaſs ; 'twill hold good ſeven Years. If you make it in Winter let it ſtand four Hours by the Fire ſhogging it. This is a very good Water.

4. *A Receipt for the Rickets.*

Take Roſemary, Bay-leaves, Camomel, Tops of Lavender, two kinds of Hay-hoes, ſowed Thyme, ſowed Hyſſop, of each of theſe one Handful, ſhred them all, and beat them in a Mortar, then boil them in a pound of ſweet freſh Butter one Hour, then ſtrain it out, and with this anoint the Child Mornings and Evenings, a quarter of an Hour together, down the Sides, and Knees, to the Feet.

5. *To make a Water good for a Surfeit, or to carry Wind or any thing off, that offends the Stomach.*

Take Hirapica one Dram, Myrrh one Dram, Scutchenele one Dram, all beaten very fine to Powder, and put it in a Quart of the beſt Anniſeed-water you can get, ſtop it cloſe, and ſet it in the Sun, and ſhake it often about that the Powders may melt, if you make it in the Winter, ſet it by the Fire and ſhake it, and drink three Spoonfuls at a time.

6. *To*

6. *To make Lozenges for a Cold.*

Take half a Pint of Colts-foot water, fo much Hyfop-water, Liquorifh three Ounces, fcrape it, and flit it thin into the Water, and let it ftand all Night, then fet it on a foft Fire; let it boil foftly, till half be confumed, then ftrain it, and put in two Ounces of brown Sugar-candy, and an Ounce of white Sugar-candy, and boil it to a Sugar: you muft keep it ftirring all the while, and when it is boiled pour it out on a Plate, and fpread it as thin as you pleafe, and then you may put it into what Shape you pleafe, there muft be no more Fire under it, than will make it boil, for if the Fire be too hot, it will turn to a Glue.

7. *To Still Rose-water.*

Wet your Rofes moift in fair Water, four Gallons of Rofes will take up near two Gallons of Water, then ftill them and take the fame Still'd Water and put it to as many frefh Rofes as it will wet, and then Still them again.

8. *A*

8. *A Receipt to cure a Consumption.*

Take a Peck of Turnips, flice them, and
lay them in Rows, and between every Row,
the Powder of Cummin, the Powder of An-
nifeeds, the Powder of Caraway, the Powder of Coriander, the Powder of the Root of
Elicampane, the Powder of Betony, of each
of thefe two Ounces, Four penny-worth of
the Powder of Saffron, put thefe in an Earthen Pot or Pan, Bake them in an Oven, and
remember before you fet it in the Oven, to
put in by the Side of the Pot, one Pint of
Hyffop water, being well baked, ftrain them,
and boil the Juice with one Pint of White-
wine, putting thereto one Ounce of *Manus
Chriftie,* three or four Ounces of the Powder of Liquorifh, one Pound of Red Sugar-
candy, ftrain it again and put it into a Pot
or Glafs, and drink thereof every Morning
and Evening, or at any other time.

9. *An approved Medicine againft the Plague.*

Take three pints of Mufcadine, Red Sage
and Rue, of each a Handful, boil them till one
pint be confumed, then ftrain it and fet it over
theFire again, then put thereto a penny worth
of long Pepper, half an Ounce of Ginger,
and a quarter of an Ounce of Nutmegs all
beaten

beaten together, then let it boil a little, and put thereto two pennyworth of Treacle, four pennyworth of Methridate, and a quarter of a Pint of the beſt Angelica-water you can get.

Keep this as your Life, above all other worldly Treaſure; take of it always warm both Morning and Evening, a Spoonful or two if you be already infected, and Sweat thereupon; if not infected, a Spoonful a day is ſufficient, half a Spoonful in the Morning and as much at Night, under God truſt to this for there never was Man, Woman or Child that ever this deceived.

This is not only good againſt the common Plague called the Sickneſs, but alſo for the Small-pox, Meazels, Surfeits, and divers other Diſeaſes.

10. *For an Ague.*

Take Bay-leaves, Red Sage, Wall-flower-leaves, (the Single if you can get them) of each a Handful, boil all theſe in a Quart of ſtrong Ale, till it come to a Pint, take half the Pint, and put into it nine Spoonfuls of Anniſeed-water, if it be for a Man; if for a Woman ſeven Spoonfuls, if for a Child three Spoonfuls, take this a little before the Fit comes.

11. *To*

11. *A Receipt of a Pomatum, which is to be made in* March, *when Marſh-mallows firſt appear.*

Take the Kidney-fat of Mutton, pick it clean from Strings or Skin: then beat it well, and work it up into thin Cakes in your Hand, ſo put them into a Pan of Spring-water: next Morning beat them again, and work them up, and put them in a freſh Water, and ſo do Morning and Night, for Nine days together; then having ready ſome new gathered Roots of Marſh-mallows, being Waſhed, ſcraped and picked, take half the Weight of the Suet, and beat them very well, then take a new Earthen-pot, well Nealed, and lay in a little of the Suet, and then the Roots, and then the Suet again: ſo cover the Pot, (not being full by a good deal) with a Cloth tied on, and an Earthen or Pewter Cover upon that, and tye down faſt: ſo ſetting it into Water with Hay, let it boil about ſix Hours, then ſtrain it out through a thin Canviſs hard, into white Earth or Silver, having a little Roſe-water in the bottom, that when it is cold it may ſlip out: when you uſe it ſcrape a little off thin with a Bone Knife, and work it ſoft in the Palm of your Hand, and ſo with your Finger rub it over your Face; and in the Morning rub it gently off with a piece of Scarlet.

A

12. *A Receipt for the Spleen.*

Take Sarſaparilla ſliced two Ounces, of
the Roots of Succory, Fearn, Polipody and
March, of each one Handful ſliced, Saſſafras
ſliced one Ounce, of the Bark of Capers
and Tamaris, bruiſed, of each one Ounce,
Juniper-berries, Bay-berries, bruiſed, of each
half an Ounce, of the Leaves of Tamaris,
Cetratch, Maiden-hair, Harts-tongue of
each one Handful ; Aſhen-keys bruiſed one
Handful ; infuſe all theſe in three Pints
of Water, and three Pints of White-wine,
in a Pipkin cloſe covered, on warm Embers
ſix Hours, and then boil it on a gentle
Fire until half be conſumed, ſtrain it out
and ſweeten it with Sugar, and put it in a
Glaſs cloſe covered, drink of this a quarter
of a Pint every Morning, and as much at
Four in the Afternoon.

N. B. Cetrach is Spleenwort, March is
Smallage.

♣♣♣♣♣:♣♣♣♣♣:♣♣:♣♣♣♣♣♣

1. *To make Spinage-Tarts.*

BOil a Quart of Milk, with a little Nutmeg, and a Stick of Cinnamon, then let it cool and beat ſix Eggs, but three Whites, and ſtir them in the Milk, and ſweeten it to your Taſte; put in a little Roſe-water, and the juice of Spinage to make it look Green, then grate two Naple-Biskets and ſtir them in, and thicken it over the Fire a little, you muſt ſtrain your Milk before you thicken it, then harden your Cuſtard before you fill them, then fill them and bake them.

2. *To make Mince-Pyes.*

Take a pound and a half of Tongue, or any other Meat you pleaſe, to make your Pyes on, Parboil it, and peel three pound of Beef-ſuet, Chop them very ſmall, and put in three pound of Currans, waſh and pick one pound of Raiſins ſtoned and chopt fine, half an Ounce of Nutmeg, half an Ounce of Mace, half an Ounce of Cinnamon beaten, and eight Pippins ſhred, two Limons ſqueezed in, and the Peel of one
ſhred

fhred fmall ; half a Pint of Sack, a quarter of a pint of Rofe-water, a quarter of a pint of White-wine or Verjuice, a pound and a quarter of Sugar, half an Ounce of Orange, and half an Ounce of Limon-peel Candied, half an Ounce of Citron, cut in little pieces; put thefe altogether with a little Salt, then fill your Pyes pretty full, and bake them in a quick Oven.

3. *To make Jumballs.*

Take two pound of fine Flour, and a pound of frefh Butter, rub it in the Flour with a pound of Sugar, put in four Eggs, but two Whites, four Spoonfuls of Rofe-water, make it up well together, and Rowl it out to what fafhion you pleafe, you may make Shrewsbury Cakes of the fame Stuff, only leave out the Seeds.

4. *Sett Cuftards.*

Let the Flour be Fine, boil your Water, then make your Pafte very ftiff and roll it out, and fet them by your Patterns, faftning it with the Whites of Eggs; then prick the Bottoms with a Pin, and wafh them with the White of an Egg, harden them in an Oven, before you fill them, and to every quart of Milk take fix Eggs, but three Whites ; boil Nutmeg

meg and whole Cinnamon, and let it be cold, then put in your Eggs, and sweeten it to your Taste, fill your Custards, and bake them in a quick Oven.

5. *A Warden Pye.*

Pare them, and bake them in an Earthen-pot, with Brown-bread, make your Pye with a quartern of Flour, and one Pound of Butter, make it Deep, and turn it into six Corners, then set the Wardens with the Tops upwards, with a few Cloves, Mace, Cinnamon, and Sugar, with some of the Syrup they are Baked in, then Close the Pye, and Bake it ; when you draw it out of the Oven, and cut up the Lidd, fill it up with a Custard, and set it into the Oven to harden : when it goes to the Table, cover it with a Lidd made of Puff-paste, stick it full of Sweat-meats.

6. *A Pottatoe Pye.*

Boil them, Peel them, Skin them, and Season them with a little Salt, beaten Cinnamon and Nutmeg, lay them into the Pye, with Yolks of Eggs boiled hard, strow Marrow, with sliced Orange and Limon-peel Candied and good store of Butter ; cut the Eggs in halves, and Marrow dipt in Yolks,

Candied

Candied Barberries, Sugar and Butter, fo clofe the Pye and bake it; then put in a Caudle of White-wine, Eggs and Sugar.

7. *To Pot a Hare.*

Take a Hare, skin it, and cut it in good big pieces, and take out the Bones, feafon the Hare, with Pepper, Salt and Nutmeg, Cloves and Mace, put it in a Pot with Butter and bake it; when it comes from the Oven, put it into a Cullender to drain; then pull it into fmall bits with your Hands before they be Cold; and knead them into Pots, and cover them with clarified Butter half an Inch thick, boil fome fat Bacon in Slices, and lay it between when you knead in the Hare; that will make it eat moift.

8. *To make Weftphalia-Ham, of a Leg of Pork.*

Take a Leg of Pork and a quarter of a Pound of Roch-petre, beat it and put to it half a Pound of brown Peter, mix them together, rub it all over the Bacon, and rub in half a Pound of brown Sugar, then cover it with a Quart of Bay-falt, and the like quantity of White Salt; when you have laid it in the Plate, after it hath lain a Week turn it every other day, it muft lye three Weeks,

then

then take it out and dry it with a Cloth, then dry it in a Stove or Chimney, you must boil it in Pump-water and Hay.

9. *To make Forc'd-meat-Balls.*

Take Veal, and cut it with a Knife, then take as much Suet, season it with Pepper, Salt, and Nutmeg, beat it first in a Mortar very fine ; shred Thyme, Savory, and sweet Marjoram, a little of each, then put in an Egg and a little Flour, and make it into Balls, some long and some round, stew them, or fry them, then strew them about the Meat, either Scotch Collops or Hashes.

10. *A Hash of Cold Meat, another Way.*

Take Gravy and Oyster-liquor, Anchovies and a Nutmeg, boil it up, then strow in your Meat, and give it a warm or two, then put in half a Pound of Butter, and half a Pint of White-wine, and send it to the Table, garnish the Dish with a Limon.

11. *To Souse Eels.*

Flea your Eels down the Back and take out the Bones, shred good store of Sweet Marjoram, Parsley and Savory, season them with Pepper, Salt and Nutmeg, then strew

the

the Herbs in the Sides of the Eels, and Roll
them up like a Collar of Bacon, put them in
a Cloth, and boil them tender with Water,
Salt and Vinegar ; when it is boiled tender,
with Spice in the Pickle, then take them out,
and when it is cold, put in your Eels, again
and keep them in it for Use.

12. *To boil a Joll of Salmon.*

Take a Bundle of Sweet Herbs, a piece of
Limon-peel, a little whole Mace, Pepper
and Nutmeg, and an Onion Stuck with
Cloves, take some Water, a Pint of Vinegar,
and some Salt, set it on the Fire with the
Herbs and Spices, and boil it well together
a good while, then boil your Fish in it, not
near a quarter of an Hour : then take it up
and set it to drain ; for Sauce, strong Broth
and Limon-peel, with two Anchovies, boil
it together, and run it through a Sieve, put
in half a Pint of Claret, a pound of Butter,
thicken it over the Fire, then lay your Fish
in the Dish, and pour your Sauce upon it,
Garnish your Dish with Limon-peel.

13. *To pickle Mushrooms.*

Take Mushrooms and pick them well,
and steep them in Water, then take ordinary Vinegar or Alligar, as much as you
think

think will cover them well, and to every
Quart of Vinegar put an Ounce of whole
Ginger white and scraped, of Jamaica Pepper half an Ounce, of White Pepper a quarter of an Ounce, as much Salt as will lie
upon half a Crown; put all these on the
Fire in a Tin thing, not in Iron, let them
boil well together for a quarter of an Hour,
put it in boiling hot on the Mushrooms, let
them stand till cold, then keep them for use
covered only with a Bit of Board, boil their
Pickle once a Month, you may put Bay-
leaves in if you please.

14. To make a Cream Cheese.

Take four Quarts of Milk, and two
Quarts of Cream, give the Cream a boil,
and so put it to the Milk, then put the Runnet to it, half a Spoonful is enough if good,
but generally they put in a Spoonful; so let
it stand, till it is very well come, about a
quarter of an Hour or rather less, then take
the Curd as whole out as you can from
the Whey, and put it in a Napkin, laid
over a Sieve, let it stand so two Hours, and
then put it into the Fat, and set fourteen
Pound weight on it, turning it every three
Hours the first Day, then take it out of the
Fat next Morning, strewing a little Salt, and
rubbing it over the Cheese, keep it in a fresh
wet

wet Cloth wrung hard Night and Morning then put it into Nettles, (but Sycamore-Leaves well wiped are better) for 10 Days, covered and shifted every Day in the Morning, then it will be fit to Eat, and after that it must be kept in Ash-boughs.

15. *To make Harts-horn Jelly.*

Take half a pound of Harts-horn, and an Ounce of Ivory, put it into a Pan, and when you have put in two Quarts of Water, measure with a Stick how deep the Water is, make a Nick on the Stick, then put in three Quarts of Water more, and cover the Pan with a Plate tyed in a Cloth, and boil it on a quick Fire, till it be boiled down to the Nick in the Stick, then strain it well thro' a Flannel-bag ; if you boil it over Night, it will be Jellied next Morning, then put it into a clean Pan or Silver Bason, and when it is melted, or just warm, put to it half a Pint of White, or half a Pint of Rhenish, and twelve Ounces of double refined Sugar, beat the Whites of four or five Eggs; you must beat the Sugar and the Eggs together ; then mix them with the Jelly, and set them on a quick Fire, put a little Civil Orange-peel to it, and let it boil 'till it cast up a thick Scum and look clear under ; then put in half a Pint of Lemon-juice, warm the Juice and strain it through a thin Cloth, then take

it

it off the Fire and strain it, Scum and all, through a Flannel Bag; let it run without pressing the Bag, then put the Bag with the Scum into another Flannel Bag, and when the Jelly is almost cold, put it into the Bag upon the Scum, for that makes it the clearer, and what drops off at first, put it in again till you find it drops very clear, then hang the Bags where they may have the Warmness of the Fire, and let them drop into the Glasses you design to serve it up in; you may boil a Sprig of Rosemary in it if you like it.

A Chadern Pye.

Boil your Chadern, then mince it small, season it with a little Cloves, Mace, and Nutmeg, a little Pepper and Salt; put in some Verjuice and Currans, a little Sugar, and grated Bread, mix all well together, put in a little Limon-peel shred small, then fill your Pye.

FINIS.

Wm Clarke
1730.

You may also be interested in these titles:

Townsends is please to make available a growing list of rare and valuable books from the 18th and early 19th centuries, including those listed below. Be sure to visit our website for a complete list of titles.

Cookbooks

The Art of Cookery by Hannah Glasse (1765)

The Domestick Coffee-Man by Humphrey Broadbent (1722) and *The New Art of Brewing Beer* by Thomas Tyron (1690)

The Complete Housewife by Eliza Smith (1730)

The Universal Cook by John Townshend (1773)

The Practice of Cookery by Mrs. Frazer (1791 & 1795)

The London Art of Cookery by John Farley (1787)

The Complete Confectioner by Hannah Glasse (1765)

A New and Easy Method of Cookery by Elizabeth Cleland (1755)

The English Art of Cookery by Richard Briggs (1788)

18th & Early 19th-Century Brewing by multiple authors

The Lady's Assistant by Charlotte Mason (1777)

The Experienced English Housekeeper by Elizabeth Raffald (1769)

The Professed Cook by B. Clermont (1769)

The Cook's and Confectioner's Dictionary by John Nott (1723)

The Modern Art of Cookery Improved by Ann Shackleford (1765)

The Country Housewife's Family Companion by William Ellis (1750)

A Collection of Above Three Hundred Receipts by Mary Kettelby (1714)

England's Newest Way in All Sorts of Cookery by Henry Howard (1726)

—⁓⁓✺⁓⁓—

Biographies & Journals

The Hessians by multiple authors

*Travels Through the Interior Parts of North-America
in the Years 1766, 1767, and 1768* by Jonathan Carver (1778)

The Women of the American Revolution, Volumes 1, 2, & 3
by Elizabeth Ellet (1848)

The Backwoods of Canada by Catharine Parr Traill (1836)

Travels into North America by Peter Kalm (1760)

New Travels in the United States of America. Performed in 1788
and *The Commerce of America and Europe*
by J.P. Brissot De Warville (1792 & 1795)

The Journal of Nicholas Cresswell, 1774–1777
by Nicholas Cresswell (1924)

An Account of the Life of the Late Reverend Mr. David Brainerd
by Jonathan Edwards (1765 & 1824)

*Travels for Four Years and a Half in the United States of America
During 1798, 1799, 1800, 1801, and 1802* by John Davis (1909)

*Travels through North and South Carolina, Georgia,
East and West Florida* by William Bartram (1792)

A Tour in the United States of America, Volumes 1 & 2
by John F. Smyth Stuart (1784)

—◦◦◦※◦◦◦—

Townsends

www.townsends.us